Luremaking

Luremaking

THE ART AND SCIENCE OF
Spinnerbaits, Buzzbaits, Jigs, and Other Leadheads

A. D. Livingston

Illustrations by
Chris Armstrong

Ragged Mountain Press
Camden, Maine

Published by Ragged Mountain Press, an imprint of TAB Books. TAB Books is a division of McGraw-Hill, Inc.

10 9 8 7 6 5 4 3 2 1

Library of Congress Cataloging-in-Publication Data
Livingston, A. D. , 1932–
    Luremaking : the art and science of spinnerbaits, buzzbaits, jigs, and other leadheads /
A.D. Livingston ; illustrations by Chris Armstrong.
      p.   cm.
    Includes index.
    ISBN 0-87742-372-5 (acid-free)
      1. Fishing lures--Design and construction.   I. Title.
SH449.L58   1994
688.7'912--dc20   93–32564
                                                          CIP

Questions regarding the content of this book should be addressed to:
Ragged Mountain Press
P.O. Box 220
Camden, ME 04843

Questions regarding the ordering of this book should be addressed to:
TAB Books
A Division of McGraw-Hill, Inc.
Blue Ridge Summit, PA 17294
1-800-233-1128

A portion of the profits from the sale of each Ragged Mountain Press book is donated to an environmental cause.
Luremaking is printed on 60-pound Renew Opaque Vellum, an acid-free paper that contains 50 percent recycled waste paper (preconsumer) and 10 percent postconsumer waste paper.

Printed by R.R. Donnelley, Harrisonburg, VA
Design by Rita Naughton
Production by Molly Mulhern
Edited by Jim Babb and Pamela Benner

Other Books by A. D. Livingston

Fishing for Bass

Advanced Bass Tackle and Boats

Fly-Rodding for Bass

Tying Bugs and Flies for Bass

Outdoor Life's *Complete Fish and Game Cookbook*

Good Vittles: One Man's Meat, a Few Vegetables, and a Drink or Two

Cast-Iron Cooking

Grilling, Smoking, and Barbecuing

Venison Cookbook

Edible Plants and Animals (with Dr. Helen N. Livingston)

For David Livingston

Contents

Foreword

There is more in this book than you suspect, even if you are a fan of A. D. Livingston and his no-nonsense approach to sportfishing. A. D. has been writing about it for many years and he hasn't repeated himself.

This is, of course, a description of luremaking and tuning, carried about as far as it can go in meticulous detail. Casual readers suddenly find themselves turning back for a second look at a passage or illustration, invariably realizing it really is the little things that count. A. D. found long ago that little things and small but important adjustments are the secret to productive lures, taking much of the luck out of fishing and making superior anglers of otherwise ordinary souls.

Understanding lures and why they do or do not work is not just a simple matter of mechanics but involves a knowledge of how and why fish strike, nibble, or refuse. Livingston has studied fish habits in depth and can go into a bass "strike" with the detail others use to describe a trout's rise. And A. D.'s bass "strike" between quotation marks because they really don't strike in the same sense as, say, a pike. Readers who have caught bass for many years may think that over a bit before accepting it.

But all of these things could be set down correctly and still come out a little dull. A. D. writes things to be read, and his sense of humor prowls just a little beneath the surface most of the time.

Angling yarns are filled with tales of lucky fishermen and lucky lures. A book like this might very well enlarge the select group of lucky anglers as well as those who won't fish with any lure they didn't make themselves—or at least improve a little. Maybe it's more fun that way.

Charles F. Waterman

Preface

Because spinnerbaits, buzzbaits, and leadhead jigs lend themselves so readily to changes in design and dressing, they fit right in with the angler's constant search for something new and hot. In addition to offering the fish something that they haven't seen before, such lures also give the tackle tinkerer literally millions of combinations to try. Color freaks will have a ball with Living Rubber skirt material, and, of course, one can experiment with various combinations of dressings, such as feathers and bucktail, and with different blades.

I believe that making and dressing leadhead lures—especially spinnerbaits—is comparable to fly tying, especially if we consider such important variables as wire design and choice of blade. New dressing materials, new paints that really stick to leadheads, an ever-increasing selection of spinner blades (counting variations in shape, size, and finish, one components manufacturer lists 3,133 different spinner blades), and the availability of inexpensive molds of good quality open up almost infinite possibilities for anglers.

I also feel that serious anglers—especially bass anglers—will profit from reading these pages and becoming familiar with design variations and possibilities, whether they make their own lures or obtain them from a custom luremaker.

A. D. Livingston

Getting Started

The most versatile fishing lure ever devised has a top-riding spinner blade and an underslung leadhead. Because the wire that connects blade and leadhead resembles an open safety pin, these lures are sometimes called safety pin spinners. Some of these, such as the popular Beetle Spin, are made with jigs and jig-spinner attachments. The best kind for the bass angler, however, has a fixed head molded onto the wire and a non-detachable blade arm. Variations on this design are numerous, but there are two basic types: single-spin and tandem-spin.

Both of these lures can be fished on top of the water, on the bottom, or anywhere in between. On the retrieve, a properly designed spinnerbait can be ripped, slow-rolled, bounced along the bottom, dropped along a ledge, buzzed on the surface, fished "stop and go," or merely cast out and cranked straight in. It's difficult to fish a spinnerbait incorrectly, and the bait, if it is of good design, is relatively trouble-free on the retrieve because it is quite snagless. It's truly a bait for all seasons.

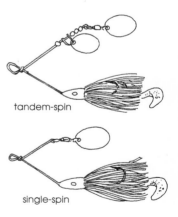

tandem-spin

single-spin

Virtually all spinnerbaits and buzzbaits are made by molding lead or heavy alloy around a hook-and-wire assembly, as shown in the drawing of a simple mold (page 2). The hook-keeper bend at the end of the wire doesn't have to be closed shut, but it does help matters if the hook and wire are pulled together under a little tension. Some people even solder the assembly together because a one-piece unit is easier to work with. I'll have more to say about this later in the book. Meanwhile, take a look at the drawing of an opened two-piece mold, showing the two halves. Such molds are usually made of aluminum. In addition to the cavities necessary to shape the leadhead, each half of the mold has slots, or channels, to hold the wire and hook in place and to allow both halves to close over the wire and the hook's shank.

Notice that the hook-and-wire assembly fits into the slots in either side of the mold, with the connection of hook and wire more or less centered in the cavity. After the hook-and-wire assembly is put in place, the two halves of the mold are closed together, and the molten lead is poured into the open-

Basic Spinnerbait Mold

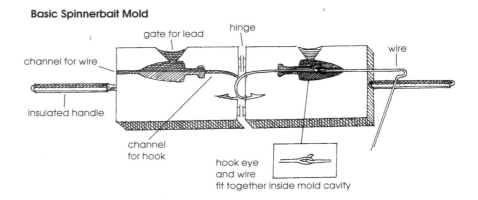

ing. (The lead can be poured from a hand-held melting unit or from a lever-operated melting pot.) The lead runs into the cavity and hardens around the hook and wire. The mold is then opened and the head is removed. Usually, the lead sprue, or waste metal, is trimmed or snipped off with a tool. Most people then "clean" each head with a knife; that is, they scrape over the spot where the sprue was removed and along the visible seams made where the two halves of the mold fit together. Clearly, the amount of cleaning depends largely on the precision and condition of the mold. Cleaning isn't really necessary in some cases, but if the mold halves don't fit together well, there is quite a bit of flashing. Even so, I've seen commercial baits that looked like they had jagged fins on the top and bottom. I've even made a few myself.

After the head has been cleaned, it is usually painted and, of course, most anglers want eyes on either side. Again, painting isn't really necessary, but most of us prefer chartreuse over the color of old lead. And eyes may actually help catch bass, although no test data are available. As Charles Waterman has said at least once in another context, only the bass know for sure—and they probably argue the point among themselves. In the world of the black bass, there are individuals everywhere, and surely the cranky smallmouth in Maine see things differently from the Texas bigmouth and those Georgia redeyes.

Be warned that cleaning leadheads may be dangerous to your health, and anyone working with raw (unpainted) heads should wash their hands thoroughly with soap and warm water before eating or handling food. I use lava soap, followed by softer suds. Safety is discussed further in Chapter 9.

In any case, after the heads have been painted and have dried, the rigging and dressing can begin. The drawing shows some of the basic possibilities. The techniques of forming and closing the loop for the swivel, attaching the blades, and tying the skirt are detailed in other chapters, along with other tricks of the trade (plus a secret or two). There is also a discussion of beads, clevises, blades, swivels, and additional rigging components.

Choices are almost infinite. Millions of combinations of dressing mate-

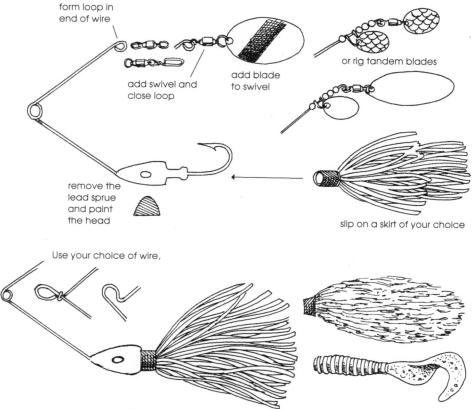

form loop in end of wire

add swivel and close loop

add blade to swivel

or rig tandem blades

remove the lead sprue and paint the head

slip on a skirt of your choice

Use your choice of wire,

or tie in dressing of Living Rubber, bucktail, etc. Use with or without a plastic or pork-rind trailer.

rials, blades, colors, and sizes are possible. Some of these variations are whims of the creator; others are important and fundamental design choices, such as the size and length of the wire—one of the more important aspects of spinnerbaits, although most anglers (and some manufacturers) never seem to consider it seriously. Such attention to detail is, of course, one of the advantages of making your own lures.

What do you need to start? Very little, really. Some tackle shops and supply houses listed in the Appendix market molded spinnerbait and buzzbait heads, either painted or raw. These can be rigged easily with swivel and blade, and can be dressed with a slip-on skirt of one kind or another. All you need are the right components and perhaps a pair of needlenose pliers.

I highly recommend, however, that you tie your own skirts from Living Rubber and get into adding other dressing materials, such as bucktail and feathers. For this you really need a good, heavy-duty fly-tying vise, a thread bobbin, and some scissors. You can get by for a while with a small bench-mounted tool vise, but don't be tempted to buy a cheap vise. You need something very sturdy for holding the head.

Of course, you may choose to use the new custom slip-on skirts, made

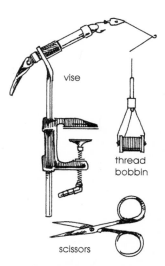

vise

thread bobbin

scissors

Essential Fly-tying Tools

with the aid of a banding machine and a collar. In this case, you'll need an inexpensive kit, but you can get by without the vise and bobbin. I personally prefer the rubber to be tied directly to the lure. I find this method not only better but also quicker and, in the long run, cheaper. Also, it permits me to add feathers, bucktail, and so on, which simply don't work with slip-on skirts.

Although the preformed heads on the market will certainly catch fish, you will probably want to get into pouring your own leadheads. For this you'll need a good mold. Fortunately, molds of good quality have become available in recent years. These are fine for starters, but remember that you can have molds custom made, or you can even make your own. Chapter 9 shows how to modify off-the-shelf molds to make such things as a spinner-bait mold from a jig mold or change the angle of the weedguard on a mold. In addition to a mold, you'll need a good lead-melting pot or an electrically heated ladle. I recommend a lead pot similar to those used for pouring bullets.

Finally, the complete do-it-yourselfer will realize that the key to successful spinnerbait and buzzbait designs is in the wire. This means that you may want to get into wire bending.

How much will all this cost? If you buy components in large quantities, it's possible to make a spinnerbait or a buzzbait for a good deal less than 50 cents in materials, but I would be pulling your leg if I said you would save money by making your own. If you're like most of us, you'll end up with an ever-increasing investment in tools and materials, just as fly tyers do. But you'll enjoy making lures at times when you can't get on the water or otherwise have cabin fever. If you're good at the craft and have an eye for detail, you'll no doubt make better lures than you can buy. At least you'll have something different, something the fish haven't seen before, something your fishing partners don't have. Besides, what's it worth to fool a trophy fish on a lure you designed and built from scratch? That's the bottom line.

Although this book covers jigs, buzzbaits, and other leadheads, it is the spinnerbait that offers more design choices and more room for personal approach. A fundamental design choice is whether you want a single-spin or a tandem-spin. As a rule, a tandem-spin works better in shallow water, and a single-spin works better in deep water. In fact, a single-spin is the choice of some expert anglers who fish for very large bass in deep water. The reason is that the blade of a well-designed single-spin turns while the bait is falling. It's no secret that many bass, especially large bass, are caught while the lure is free-falling. Some jig experts tie in a bulky skirt just to slow down the fall, sometimes calling it an umbrella jig or a parachute jig. The blade on a properly designed single-spin works even better for this purpose, giving the bait a slower fall rate as well as providing some vibration and flash.

I believe that controlling the fall rate is, by far, the more important function of the blade on a single-spin. An impeccably designed lure not only brings more "strikes" from lunker bass but also permits the angler to detect

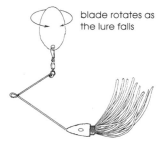

blade rotates as the lure falls

them. Let me explain. A black bass (largemouth, smallmouth, spotted, or redeye) doesn't "strike" a lure and doesn't grab hold of it like a pike or a garfish does. A bass opens its bucket mouth and gill flaps, creating a suction, and the lure (or bait) is literally sucked in with a rush of water. The fish can also reverse the flow, blowing out the lure in an instant. Time and again, underwater photography has shown that bass have taken a lure and spit it out without the angler ever knowing it. This is especially true with a fall bait, which goes down on more-or-less slack line or at least on line that isn't being reeled in fast. (Underwater photography has shown that bass can even engulf and blow out a crankbait plug with treble hooks sticking out from it, without the angler ever realizing that he had had a "bite.") Believe it or not, the spinnerbait can help the angler detect these strikes.

How? First, let me say that the angler must have everything just right and finely tuned: the right weight for the spinnerbait head, the right wire in the right proportion (the length of the blade arm in relation to the underslung leadhead arm), the right swivel, the right blade, the right line, and the right rod. And the right frame of mind. As the bait falls, the angler follows it down by feel. The blade spins, causing a throb that can be felt with a sensitive rod; if everything is right, the rod tip will dance a little. Usually, a rod made of graphite, boron, or some other modern-age material works best. Also, a one-piece rod blank that goes through the handle is better than a jointed rod that is fitted into a handle. What happens, of course, is that the angler stays in touch with his lure by feeling the vibration of the blade. When he doesn't feel the blade working, he strikes immediately to set the hook, knowing that a lunker bass may have engulfed his lure and can spit it out just as quickly. Be warned that this is serious fishing, requiring the ultimate in balanced tackle and concentration. In addition to feeling for the blade, the angler who is more "lucky" than his fellows will be watching the line carefully, knowing that a minute twitch may indicate that a bass has taken the lure. He'll catch fish while his partner is watching the osprey swoop, scratching a chigger, enjoying the sunset, or cussing at water-skiers.

The importance of the sense of feel is not limited to deep-water fishing. Even in shallow water, the throb of the blade helps keep the angler in touch with his lure and lets him know that all is well. At night, you need such reassurance. In this regard, a buzzbait (covered in other chapters) or some such noisemaker like the Jitterbug plug also helps. Further, the savvy shallow-water angler knows that the bait can be pulled in at just the right speed, keeping the blade just under the surface, so that it makes a wake in the water. This technique usually works better with tandem-spins, but perfectly balanced single-spins will do. I also use a rig that I call a Wake Bait, which has no swivel. In any case, this technique can be deadly in early morning, late afternoon, and at night.

Although the spinner blade's flash may be important in some cases, and surely the blade's vibration will attract such fish as largemouth bass (which locate their prey primarily by sensing vibrations in the water), I feel that the angler will increase his catch significantly if he will always consider his spinner blade not as a fish attractor but as a communication device capable of keeping him in touch with his lure.

Having said all that, I might add that the spinnerbait doesn't have to be taken quite so seriously, and often bass can be caught by merely casting the lure out and cranking it back in. Although I am aware that a properly designed single-spin worked in deep water is usually the better way to catch larger bass, I really do prefer, most of the time, to fish with a tandem-spin in shallow water. I also enjoy casting to visible cover, whether I catch fish or not. The object of the game is to come as close as possible to a stump or cypress knee or, better, to throw the lure up under an overhanging bush without getting hung up. A spinnerbait (especially the in-line design) is a good choice for this kind of casting because the skirt provides a little air resistance, aiding in the presentation. Further, the do-it-yourselfer who dresses his own spinnerbaits has the best of it because he can control the amount and type of material that goes into the skirt.

Fine points aside, even those people who merely cast out a spinnerbait and crank it in almost without thinking—until a bass erupts—need a bait that runs true and catches fish when they strike. Poorly designed spinnerbaits miss far too many strikes. This is especially true of buzzbaits, some of which seem designed to keep the bass from getting hooked. Frankly, I would no more fish with some commercial baits I've seen than I would jump off the top of a house.

Spinnerbait Wire

Although each spinnerbait must have a blade, head, and skirt of reasonable size and proper proportion, the secret of a successful design lies largely in the selection and engineering of the wire. The first requirement of the wire is that it not rust. A fellow of my acquaintance who imported some 20,000 spinnerbait heads from Mexico knows exactly why. The wire started rusting before the spinnerbaits ever left the tackle shops. It's best to pay for top-quality stainless steel wire and stick with it.

The wire must connect blade, lure, and line together. The point where the line is knotted to the wire is called the eye. On most spinnerbaits with top-riding blades, the eye can be open or closed, with several variations of both kinds. (Eyes for in-line spinnerbaits and buzzbaits are covered in other chapters.)

The strongest connection is the closed, or twisted, eye, as shown in the drawing (page 8). A line tied to such an eye will hold to knot strength without breaking or altering the wire in any way. Also, the twisted eye permits the use of small-diameter spinnerbait wire. (Wire diameter will be discussed later in this chapter.) The twisted eye also works better for those anglers who prefer to use a snap, snap swivel, or split ring in the eye. The purpose of a snap, of course, is to permit rapid changing of lures, a convenience that many anglers want. Another purpose of a snap or a split ring is to permit free movement of the spinnerbait, without the binding effect caused by a knot. Obviously, a snap or ring of any sort cannot be used satisfactorily in an open bend. The ring or snap is certain to run up the wire to the blade, or down the wire to the head, on the cast or during retrieves in heavy cover. In this regard, a closed loop is highly desirable.

The big disadvantage of the twisted-eye loop is that the angler's line sometimes wraps around the wire. This usually happens on a sloppy cast, or when the lure flops around in grass or heavy cover. When the line is fouled, the lure may not run straight. Worse, a fouled line pinches and binds in the V, resulting in reduced line strength. In short, the twisted eye

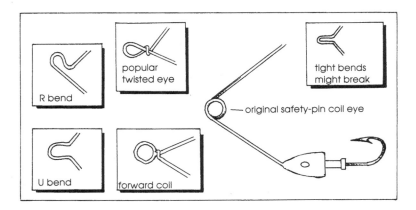

can cause the line to break and a big fish to be lost.

Some purists don't like twisted eyes because they throw the lure out of alignment by the diameter of the wire. This can be compensated for by hand-bending the wire slightly during rigging or by tuning before and during fishing.

The so-called R bend becomes popular here and there from time to time, and it has a definite following of anglers who will fish with nothing else. The main advantage is that the line doesn't wrap around the twisted wire and bind in a V, since the connection is open. If the line wraps around the blade arm on the cast, the knot merely turns around when pressure is applied. The obvious disadvantage of the open eye is that it can cause problems when used with snaps or rings, as discussed above.

Some other open bends crop up from time to time. The R is by far the most common because it can be made with one operation on a wire-bending tool. The other basic design, a U, requires two bending operations, and for this reason it is seldom used on commercial spinnerbaits, where every fraction of a penny counts.

The loop, or coil eye, which is really a short coil spring, has a good number of followers, and it is indeed a good design. It can be made in a wire-bending tool, but not many commercial baits use this design. I like it, partly because it combines some of the benefits of the twisted eye: it is closed and can be used with light wire and a snap. Also, the coil doesn't cut off fouled line as readily as a twisted eye does.

Usually, the loop or coil is made so that the eye resembles the end of a safety pin. Sometimes I form the coil forward, but this is a very unconventional eye and anyone who considers using it commercially ought to first do some market research. Although it is not generally known or widely considered, the choice of line tie or eye design should depend, in part, on the diameter of the wire being used. The very heavy wire (0.051-inch diameter) normally used on buzzbaits is seldom seen in a twisted eye because of mechanical difficulties in manufacture. Also, the resulting offset would be a bit much for eye appeal and balance. Normally, wire no greater than 0.040 inch in diameter is used in a twisted eye.

Some good anglers want a light wire because it produces more blade action, or what I call blade swing. A wide swing of the top arm permits an exaggerated blade motion, and probably transmits action to the bottom arm and skirt. Such a swing might also transmit more vibration up the line to the angler. This vibration can be very important to some anglers, especially those who fish the spinnerbait as a fall bait in deep water. In any case, the blade swing is more pronounced with light wire.

Nonetheless, it may be unwise to use light wire with *any* open bend because blade swing causes repeated stress at the line-tie point, which can cause the wire to break, just as repeated bending of any wire can cause failure. Remember, the stress point is also at a place where the outer edge of the wire is already stretched severely by the bend. (If you start with a straight wire and put a bend in it, the outside edge of the bend has to stretch, whereas the inside of the bend is under compression.) In short, the bend itself weakens the line-tie point, and the repeated action of the blade swing slowly aggravates the problem.

I have had breaks occur at the line-tie point, and for that reason I have quit fishing with R or U bends in wire less than 0.040 inch in diameter. On the other hand, I want to point out that the lures I broke had relatively tight bends, or a small U. The tighter the bend, the more the stress is concentrated and the more likely a break will occur.

In conclusion, I recommend that wire used with a twisted eye or coil eye be 0.035 inch in diameter for ¼-ounce and ⅜-ounce heads; ⅛-ounce heads can go down to 0.029; and ½-ounce heads can go up to 0.040. Open bends should not be made in wire smaller than 0.040.

Another consideration is what I call hook bite, or gap; this point is foremost in my personal approach to spinnerbait design. By hook bite, I mean the clearance that allows the fish to get at the hook.

With double-spins, which are normally (but not always) fished in shallow water, the fish comes up and hits the bait from beneath, thereby miss-

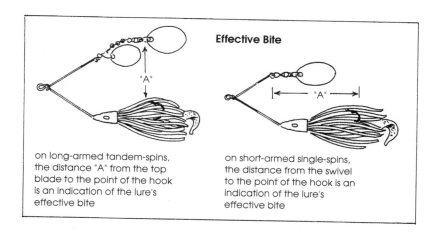

Effective Bite

on long-armed tandem-spins, the distance "A" from the top blade to the point of the hook is an indication of the lure's effective bite

on short-armed single-spins, the distance from the swivel to the point of the hook is an indication of the lure's effective bite

ing the top-riding blades. In other words, the fish goes for the skirt and, hopefully, doesn't get the blades in its mouth. This means that the lure's bite is determined by the vertical distance from the blade down to the hook's point. On the other hand, if the blades are too close to the hook, the fish is more likely to get the whole works into its mouth, which can present problems in setting the hook.

A single-spin's bite is different, and is determined by the horizontal distance between the hook point and the top-blade wire. The blade itself can swing down without touching the hook's point and therefore will have no practical bearing on the bait's hooking ability. If a large fish gets the entire lure in its mouth, the wire would have to bend down before the fish could be hooked. Of course, it's entirely possible to bend the wire down when setting the hook. The point is that you'll miss fish from time to time because the wire acts as a hook guard. For this reason, it's best to have the blade well forward of the hook's point so that the fish will close down between the end of the blade arm and the hook's point.

I am aware that my thinking on this matter runs counter to some lure designs. Once, I sold lots of spinnerbaits to a tackle shop in Georgia. The bait sold better than any spinnerbaits the store had ever handled, but the owner, a tournament fisherman, wanted something *different*. Change for change's sake, I call it. He showed me some of my baits that he had modified considerably. To do this, he had untwisted the eye and put a new twist closer to the head. Since this was obviously lots of trouble when done bait by bait, he wanted me to manufacture the altered version for him. When I asked him why he wanted the eye closer to the head, he knew only that he tried it and liked the short arm and believed that it caught lots of fish for him. "In one tournament," he said, "I caught a limit on it and would have won the money if I hadn't missed two 7-pounders that hit right at the boat." So there you have it. If he had been fishing with a long-arm bait, he might well have caught the two lunkers. But what I said to him didn't matter, and what I say here won't matter either whenever someone thinks they've got a hot new design.

I'll say it anyhow: Dozens of hotshot new spinnerbaits come and go, but the old classic design survives and catches bass and other gamefish year after year. The basic proportions for this bait, both single-spin and double-spin, are shown in the drawing at left and at the top of page 11.

In the drawing for a single-spin, L is the distance from the end of the line tie to the eye of the hook or the hook keeper in the wire. I recommend that L be from 25 to 35 percent longer than H, where H is the length of the hook. (These proportions are based on the short-shank hook normally used in spinnerbaits, such as the Eagle Claw 253. Note that changing H, or hook styles, will change the other dimensions. Note also that changing the size of the 253 hook will alter the other dimensions somewhat. So be careful. Don't use this rule of thumb as a rigid formula, unless Eagle Claw 253 hooks are used in reasonable sizes. Of course, the 3/0 size is usually used with ¼- and ⅜-ounce baits, 4/0 or 5/0 with ½-ounce or larger baits, and 2/0 with ⅛-ounce baits.)

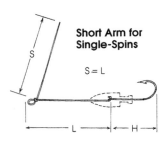

Short Arm for Single-Spins

S = L

The distance S is the length of the spinner-blade arm, as measured *before* the swivel-keeper loop is formed in the wire, for typical single-spin baits. I recommend that S be equal to L or perhaps 10 percent shorter than L. This depends somewhat on how large the swivel-keeper loop will be. (Forming this loop is discussed in Chapter 5.)

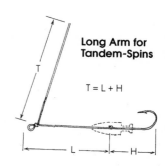

Long Arm for Tandem-Spins

T = L + H

For double-spin baits, I recommend that L be the same as for single-spins, but that T be much longer than S. Roughly, T should equal L + H. Thus, if you bend the wire arm of a tandem spinnerbait straight back, before rigging with blades and swivel, the end of the wire should touch the bend of the hook.

A good many hobbyists, and even some manufacturers, split the difference by using the same length wire for the top arm of both single and tandem spinnerbaits. Usually, they choose a blade arm halfway between the classic single-spin and the classic tandem-spin. In so doing, they get by with using only one wire for both types of lures, thereby simplifying inventory. But they lose something in both kinds of spinnerbaits, not only in how the baits run in the water but also in the number of fish they catch— or miss.

Still another design, which is not very popular, makes use of a sort of swivel-joint wire. This design can be used with a single-spin or a tandem-spin. In fact, baits of this design, rigged with two blades, have been touted as the tandem-spin that can be fished as a fall bait. The implication is that the small front blade, rigged on a clevis, turns while the lure is falling. It doesn't. It won't. At least not for me—unless you've got a very heavy head rigged with a small blade. In any case, the design has merit, but the joint tends to pick up moss and trash, and is, in general, untidy.

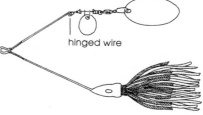

hinged wire

Most anglers, and I am certainly no exception, will want to inspect a spinnerbait's wire and bend it by hand this way or that before fishing with it. This is partly a visible check in alignment, making sure that the blade or blades are centered over the hook point. Most of us also adjust the angles of the wire somewhat.

I recommend that the wire from the head to the line-tie eye be bent up from 35 to 45 degrees. Also, the angle between the two wires should be from 80 to 90 degrees, at least with spinnerbaits with wire of normal length. (Long, limber wire, such as used on the Bagley Switch Blade bait, would have a narrow angle.)

Personally, I prefer the angles to be 45 and 90 degrees, sharp, but I emphasize that this is a personal preference. Once I handed one of my tandem-spins, which I considered to be well-nigh perfect, to Carl Wingo, an expert angler in Virginia, who is noted for frequent catches of very large bass on spinnerbaits. The first thing he did was bend the wire down so that the blades were only an inch or so above the hook's point! I'll also have to point out that most of his large fish were taken on single-spins, which he said he preferred. I think I know why!

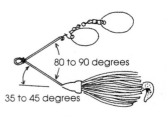

80 to 90 degrees

35 to 45 degrees

◇ ◇ ◇

coil-spring tandem-spin

Finally, mention must be made of other aspects of spinnerbait wire and off-beat designs. Some of these come and go every year, and some are bound to be back in vogue from time to time. Consider the spring-wire design. The first ones I ever saw came from Jim Rodgers, who I haven't heard from in years. I bought quite a few of these, and still have some, from a fellow named Hank Trent in California. (No, I don't have a current source of these baits, or of the spring wire itself.)

In any case, spring arms, if that's the term, are usually used with tandem-spins, and have a small wire diameter, partly because of the increased difficulty in making coil springs in the larger wire. These are usually very limber arms, and do indeed have good action and wide blade swing. The only problem, apart from increased cost, is that the spring coil collects too much trash and tends to hang up more than ordinary wire.

A few years before I wrote this book, my telephone was ringing off the hook with folks wanting *tapered* spinnerbait wire. I didn't have any and still don't. I've never quite understood the need for tapered wire, but I suspect it had something to do with strength in an R or U bend, along with the limberness of light wire on the blade arm. In any case, the wire tapered from heavy diameter—from the eye out—to lighter wire at the end of the blade arm. I have heard some complaints about the wire breaking, although I have no personal experience with this design.

Limbernecks, as they're called, require the use of wire combined with either stiff monofilament line or steel leader material (or steel encased in plastic). Although this design was popular for a spell, I don't expect the lure ever to dominate the market; the thing is just untidy from a mechanical and aesthetic viewpoint. First, the limber arm has to be connected to the wire arm just above the eye, and then some sort of loop must be made in the limber arm to hold the swivel. Usually, crimped leader sleeves are used for these connections.

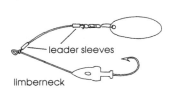

leader sleeves

limberneck

How limber is it? Frankly, I don't know. I've heard that one big advantage of this design is that it enables both blades on a tandem-spin to turn while the lure is sinking. I've experimented with this, but it just doesn't work, at least not for me. In any case, anyone interested in this design should do some further research for patents. I saw an ad once in a magazine that claimed that some manufacturer had exclusive rights to this design. I might add that design patents not involving secret materials are hard to enforce, but, I hasten to add, I am not a lawyer.

One of the very best fish-catching spinnerbait designs is quite old and was one of the first commercially made lures with top-riding spinner blades. (This bait, made by Shannon Lure Company, was usually dressed with bucktail.) I've seen several newer twin-spins, but the problem is in getting two pieces of wire out of the line-tie eye. Another design has a sort of collapsible weedguard wire attachment, which was somewhat shaky in my opinion. I've also seen a V-wire soldered to a short wire at the eye. This is my choice, but the design requires more handwork, which in turn shoots up the price.

One minor problem for the angler is that the twin-spin design is hard to fit compactly into a tackle box. A major problem for those who market lures is that twin-spins are difficult to package and ship. Another problem is that doing battle with fish and stumps tends to bend the wires every which way, so that frequent tuning is necessary.

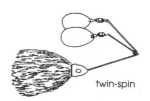

twin-spin

I've seen some spinnerbaits, made, I believe, by Fred Arbogast some time ago, that had a twin-blade arm installed about halfway up the blade arm. This was accomplished by first affixing a metal tube, similar to a leader sleeve, crosswise on the main arm. A wire was then run through this tube; both ends of the wire were bent back and allowed to swing freely. Small blades were attached to the end of the wire with swivels. I don't see a big advantage to such a rig, except possibly it keeps the hook from getting tangled from the side. I have made such a lure successfully by wrapping a leader sleeve in place with fine copper wire and filling in with solder. Such a rig requires lots of work, and three swivel rigs—important considerations for the manufacturer, but not necessarily for the do-it-yourselfer.

triple-spin

Willowleaf tandem-spins have been popular in parts of Florida and Louisiana for many years, and in 1986 very large willow blades, sometimes called Okeechobee blades, became something of a craze. Even size 7 and 8 blades were in great demand, and the host of a TV fishing show looked me up, thinking I might have some. I told him to use the top of an anchovy can, but he was going tournament fishing and wasn't in any mood for joking around. Anyhow, these large blades hang far behind the hook, making for an untidy lure. I designed a new wire especially for willow blades, and it puts everything in better perspective. Anyone who believes that bass "nip" at blades should consider this design carefully. Because the wire is longer than usual, I recommend that nothing smaller than 0.040 wire be used in a twisted eye. This bait is also rigged in an unconventional way, having an extra dogleg in the wire. I put the dogleg in the wire design to help shed moss and grass off the clevis and swivel.

Livingston's long-wire willow-spin

Some manufacturers and hobbyists put a different sort of dogleg in willow-spins, partly as a convenient stop for the smaller blade. Such a bait is shown in the drawing at right. Also note that some people put some sort of a kicker bend in the lower arm, but I've never seen a winning argument for such an extra bend; I feel it's merely change for the sake of change—reason enough to sell millions of new lures every year.

Still another spinnerbait, with a head shaped like a banana jig, is quite popular in some quarters, especially in areas of Louisiana and Texas. It has been manufactured for years by the H&H Lure Company. I've seen other similar lures, called His and Her, or some such name. In any case, these lures are unique in that they have a wire loop, an extension of the regular wire, that sticks out the rear end. A hook, usually a double, is attached to the

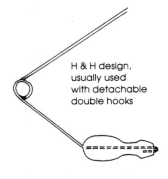

H & H design, usually used with detachable double hooks

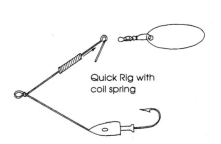

Quick Rig with coil spring

loop. The rubber skirt, bucktail, or other dressing is put on the banana-head body. This design almost always has rather heavy wire and a coil eye. I don't care for the H&H design—but a lot of bass and other gamefish have had other opinions over the years.

Once I marketed, under the name of Quick Rig, a spinnerbait head that used an open loop on the blade end of the wire. A coil spring was put onto the wire, ahead of the open loop; the end of the swivel was hooked on over the wire. To rig the thing, the arm of the wire was depressed and the coil spring was slipped down over the wire, closing the opening. Thus, it could be rigged without pliers or tools. It sold pretty well, owing entirely to its quick-rig feature, but the fellow who made it for me discontinued the head and, shortly thereafter, got out of the spinnerbait trade and into the wildcat oil business. Before making the move he told me that the open loop tangled so badly—both before and after it was molded into the head—that he wouldn't manufacture any more quick rigs at any price. I dropped the design, partly because the spring wire and open loop made an untidy connection and picked up moss and silt from the water.

Of course, the hobbyist can make good use of quick rigs, but anyone who sets up to market lures might remember that any sort of loop on the end of the blade arm will cause tangles. Although such loops might well speed up part of the rigging, the time saved should be measured carefully against the time lost in untangling wire before and after the lure is poured and painted. A fellow in California once made 2,000 quick-rig baits (with a simple loop in the end of the wire) and tossed them, one by one, into a box as they came out of the mold. It took him a week to untangle them. In any case, any sort of quick rig is suitable only for a single-spin bait.

Every year I think I've seen the last quirk in spinnerbait design, but somebody always surprises me. Once, for example, a tool and die maker sent me a spinnerbait made with a jig hook. The firm called it Direct Concept, claiming great things for the vibrations the angler felt from it. I fished with the new bait, but, in all honesty, I didn't feel what they were talking about.

My objection to the design is that the apex of the bait must be shaped like a rod guide in order for the line to go through it. This is not ideal for pulling through grass and heavy cover. My biggest objection, however, is that the jig hook doesn't have enough bite.

This lack of bite is true of all jigs, as well as keel flies, simply because of the shape of the hook. The jig hook works well enough when bounced slowly—stop-and-go fashion—along the bottom, so that the bass engulfs it on a relatively slack line. It's another matter for a spinnerbait that is fished fast.

In addition to the hooking problem, flexible-joint jig spinnerbaits are not as weedless or snagless as regular spinnerbaits, on which the wire and blade arm act as weedguards for the rigid head. Because the jig is flexible on the wire harness, it flops over and hooks onto limbs, grass, and so on.

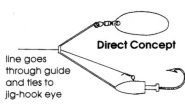

Direct Concept

line goes through guide and ties to jig-hook eye

jig-spinner attachment

The jig-spinner design, does, however, run straight and is deadly on crappie, bluegill, rock bass, and smaller trout. I've caught lots of largemouth and smallmouth bass on such a lure, but it will never replace the conventional spinnerbait head and wire design. For one reason, most anglers, myself included, don't trust the snap-on arrangement of the jig-spinner design when we're going after bass, muskie, and other gamefish larger than a crappie or a bluegill. For one thing, the wire is usually pretty flimsy. Of course, the complete do-it-yourselfer can form jig spinners out of heavier wire. Still, I don't recommend the design because the jig itself is not a good hooker. This is especially true of weedless jigs.

A perfectly balanced spinnerbait will run straight at a very fast retrieve. This ideal can be accomplished if wire length, head weight, and choice of blade are selected with balance in mind. I can put together a spinnerbait that will run straight up when retrieved as fast as you can crank, even with modern high-speed reels. But it might not be an ideal bait for fishing because the blades wouldn't be large enough.

Generally, the smaller the blade, the easier it is to balance a bait. Those who want large blades on light heads have a problem and must compromise. Usually, the knowledgeable angler will go ahead and use the blade of his choice, knowing full well that the bait will tilt sideways if he retrieves it too fast. Sometimes adjustments can be made. Rick Clunn, if I remember correctly, won a major bass tournament on Guntersville Lake by fishing very large size 8 Colorado blades on his spinnerbaits. To help balance the bait, Clunn pinched additional lead sinkers around the wire, just above his spinnerbait head.

The problem of balance is discussed further in chapters 3 and 4, on head design and blade choice. The point here is that the length of the wire, top and bottom, and the proportion of top and bottom lengths, have a good deal to do with balance. Consider the drawings on page 16.

When a blade turns, either clockwise or counterclockwise, it tends to pull the spinnerbait over on its side. This force, or torque, is counterbalanced to some degree by the weight of the leadhead. If the blade is too big or the head is too light, or the rate of retrieve is too fast, the bait will turn on its side. Sometimes this can be corrected by bending the wire a little (tuning) or by slowing down the retrieve. Of course, design changes also help. As a rule, the farther the head is from the line of pull, the straighter the bait will run. Also, the closer the blade is to the line of retrieve, the straighter the bait will run, other things being equal. Thus, spinnerbaits with identical heads and blades will run differently. This is merely a shift of mass and torque caused by using wire of different lengths for the blade arm and the head arm.

It has been said, quite correctly, that the spinnerbait is the most versatile of all fishing lures. It should have become obvious to anyone reading these pages that the spinnerbait is also a lure of infinite variety and subtle varia-

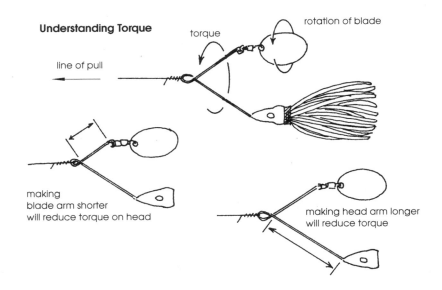

Understanding Torque

line of pull

torque

rotation of blade

making
blade arm shorter
will reduce torque on head

making head arm longer
will reduce torque

tions, owing largely to the selection and shaping of the wire. Being so parametric, the spinnerbait design is full of pitfalls for the novice tackle tinkerer. It can also be a quagmire for perfectionists. But the contemplative angler, willing to compromise one feature for advantages in another, can usually come up with a bait to do pretty much what he wants it to do, whether it be bouncing along the bottom during the heat of a summer day, spin-dropping along a ledge, or burbling the water's surface in the dark of night.

Heads and Hooks

The head does several things for a spinnerbait or buzzbait: it provides weight for casting; it encases the hook and wire connection; and it provides an area for paint and eyes, adding to the lure's attraction—at least to the fisherman, and maybe even to the bass. Finally, it provides a base on which to tie a skirt, or incorporates a keeper to hold a slip-on rubber or vinyl skirt.

Although there are notable exceptions, most spinnerbait heads are shaped more or less like a bullet. This design is pleasing to the eye, it makes a streamlined connection with the wire, it goes through weeds smoothly, it takes an eye nicely, and it looks like something.

With buzzbaits, however, the trend is to flatten the head. At least in theory, a flat head rides higher for a given rate of retrieve, which permits the angler to keep the bait on top with a slower retrieve. Almost all buzzbait heads are a little flat, and can be flattened further by beating them with a hammer. That's right. Put the head on an anvil and tap on it. The paint may chip off, but some modern paints may hold up under considerable pounding. Anyone who wants to make large numbers of flatheads by squeezing them down should invest in a good arbor press.

Too much flattening tends to cock the leadhead on the wire, simply because each piece of wire has a hook keeper that sticks up. Buzzbait wires usually cause more problems because they are heavier.

Usually, heads for spinnerbaits, buzzbaits, and jigs are made of lead or an alloy containing lots of lead. In addition to being readily available, lead has a low melting point and "pours" easily; that is, it works pretty well in a mold. Be warned, however, that there is a move afoot to ban lead in fishing tackle. This topic is discussed further in chapters 9 and 14, and in the Epilogue.

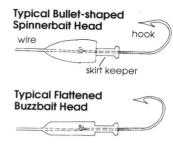

Typical Bullet-shaped Spinnerbait Head

wire   hook

skirt keeper

Typical Flattened Buzzbait Head

WEIGHT

Most spinnerbait heads fall within the range of ⅛-, ¼-, ⅜-, and ½-ounce, with ¼- and ⅜-ounce heads being by far more popular than the others. Buzzbaits follow pretty much the same size pattern. (Jigs, however, range from several ounces down to 1/32 or even 1/64 ounce.) Spinnerbait weight is often determined by the angler's preference for casting line and equipment; a ⅛-ounce bait works best with a light rig, whereas a ½-ounce bait requires a stiffer rod for proper casting. Apart from castability, the depth at which one intends to fish is sometimes very important. As more and more fishermen learn the art of fishing a spinnerbait in deep water, heads have become larger, so that today we see increasing demand for ¾- and even 1-ounce sizes. These will handle large blades, and are easier to feel when the lure free-falls.

For buzzbaits, ultralight fans will want a ⅛-ounce head; others will prefer ¼- or ⅜-ounce sizes, which will take a larger, noisier blade. There are some ½-ounce baits on the market, but I, for one, have never had any use for them—although I quickly add that one of the all-time best-selling buzzbaits has a ½-ounce head.

Also, ½-ounce baits can be cast farther, which can be an important consideration because the buzz blade is highly wind resistant. Catalogs often describe buzz blades according to the size of head they're designed to accompany. A tiny buzz blade won't keep a 1-ounce lure on top unless the retrieve is very fast, and of course most anglers want to slow down the retrieve instead of speeding it up. But a very large blade on a tiny head will cause the bait to run off to the side instead of tracking straight. A compromise is necessary, and that's the nice thing about making your own lures.

Before quitting the subject of head weight, I must point out that there is no standard in the fishing-tackle industry, and no manufacturer, to my knowledge, specifies whether the listed weight includes blades, rigging hardware, and skirt, or whether the weight applies only to the head and wire. In any case, some "¼-ounce" heads weigh closer to ⅜ ounce, and some billed as ⅜-ounce are closer to ½ ounce. Further, some of the lures made in rubber molds get larger, and maybe even become lopsided, after the mold has been in use for a long time.

So much for weight. Here are a few other topics to consider.

SKIRT KEEPER

Surprisingly, a leadhead's skirt keeper can be quite important. If it does what it's supposed to do, everything's fine. If it doesn't, the skirt will slip off or slip back into the bend of the hook. The skirt keeper should be large enough in diameter to hold a slip-on skirt—but not so large that it makes the slip-on too difficult. Usually, modern rubber skirts, which are glued around a short length of surgical tubing, are fairly easy to slip on, but vinyl skirts don't have as much stretch. Also, some of the new filament skirts made with tiny rubber O-rings or collars are difficult to slip onto large skirt keepers.

If the head will be used with hand-tied Living Rubber skirts, it should have a skirt keeper designed especially for holding the rubber in place. If it doesn't, thread must be built up behind it to prevent slipping, which can involve lots of thread winding. I believe that I designed the first skirt keeper of this sort, and it has been used on other baits since then.

Regular Collar. The skirt keeper shown here is the classic design for lead-heads intended to be used with a slip-on skirt. This design is standard on most commercial molds, and is often used with hand-tied skirts as well as with slip-ons. Some people who specialize in leadheads with Living Rubber skirts make a cut into the skirt keeper to hold the thread or wire, preventing the whole works from slipping back. This technique can be used for making a few baits, but it is too time-consuming for mass production.

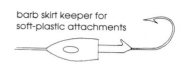

collar skirt keeper
for slip-on skirts

Worm or Grub Keeper. This design is standard on many jigs that are intended to be fished with plastic worms or grubs, and it is also used on some spinnerbait heads. If you like to fish with grubs as trailers, remember that it is possible to use an extended skirt keeper, making use of both the slot feature and the barb.

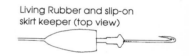

barb skirt keeper for
soft-plastic attachments

Living Rubber Keeper. David Livingston and I came up with this shape back in 1980 or thereabouts, to help hold Living Rubber skirts in place. The idea was to wind the thread in part of the slot, then tie the rubber down in front of the thread. Ideally, the slot kept the thread from slipping back. The first turn of thread around the rubber forced it down into the slot in front of the thread (the rubber touched the leadhead), making a very tight wrap that would not slip (discussed in more detail under the section on Living Rubber). This design isn't available on most commercial molds, but it can be made by modifying the mold, as described in Chapter 9.

Living Rubber and slip-on
skirt keeper (top view)

Tony's Safe Keeper. An ingenious fellow by the name of Tony came up with a skirt keeper that I like very much, and we used it in a line of baits that we marketed some time ago. The shape of the skirt keeper is shown at right, and it can be used in most commercial molds if you are handy with tools. (See Chapter 9.)

Tony's Safe Keeper (top view)

THE HOOK

Spinnerbait hooks are usually short shanked and have a small eye. Small eyes have several advantages, especially if you are molding lots of heads. First, a small eye simply fits better with the spinnerbait wire; the unit "lays down" better when you put it into the mold. Second, the small eye contains less metal to cool and harden the molten lead; it's easier to "pour" with a small-eyed hook. Third, a hook with a small eye is much easier to untangle in a box of bulk hooks simply because the barb of one hook doesn't stick through the eyelet of another.

Style. I consider the Eagle Claw 253 to be the standard hook for spinner-baits and buzzbaits, although I would prefer a longer shank. Some new spinnerbait hooks, such as the 255, do have longer shanks. If I were going to manufacture spinnerbaits and buzzbaits for the market, I would stick with the 253 or 255 design, or similar designs.

If I were going to make a few baits for my personal use, however, I would look for a longer-shank hook made with lighter wire, and would probably settle for an Aberdeen. Since its smaller diameter makes the Aberdeen easier to set, I would consider going up a size larger than standard. The Aberdeen's long shank is also an advantage for those of us who don't like trailer hooks.

One problem with hook selection is that most commercial molds specify a certain kind of hook and a certain size. But I always feel free to cut and file and fill and otherwise modify any mold that I paid for. Fortunately, good molds are relatively inexpensive these days, so that ruining one with a hacksaw and file from time to time isn't a disaster.

Size. These are standard hook sizes for baits using Eagle Claw 253 and 255 hooks: ⅛-ounce, 2/0; ¼-ounce, 3/0; ⅜-ounce, 3/0 or 4/0; ½-ounce, 4/0; for larger spinnerbaits, 5/0. Not many years ago, some of the tournament anglers and TV hosts were plugging baits with what I consider to be over-sized hooks. Their thinking was that these hooks had more bite and therefore caught more fish. But I feel that many anglers have trouble setting a large hook, especially if they are fishing long casts with a limber rod and a monofilament line with lots of stretch. Personally, I don't want to fish a 5/0 253 hook with standard bass tackle. If I were to do so, I would sharpen the point very carefully.

Finish. Because the hook is usually more or less hidden by the skirt, I don't attach much importance to finish; a standard nickel-plated hook is fine with me. Others prefer bronze. Some insist on gold-plated hooks, especially around brackish or salt water, since gold-plated hooks don't rust as badly as some other hooks. However, sharpening any plated hook will expose the base metal and make it susceptible to rust. Anyone who fishes spinnerbaits in brackish water ought to look into hooks made from stainless steel or other rustless material.

The Trailer Hook

Let me say first of all that I don't believe in using a trailer hook at all, unless the spinnerbait or buzzbait is designed in such a way that a bass or other fish has to work at getting hooked. Quickly I add that I seem to be in the minority on this matter. All the TV fishermen I've seen, as well as some tournament anglers and magazine writers, swear by trailer hooks, claiming they help take those "short strikes." There may be such a thing as a short strike, but, really, the notion isn't in keeping with the way in which a bass engulfs a lure. I *have* seen a small pickerel grab a spinnerbait by the skirt—repeatedly—but a bass doesn't nip at skirts or blades. It's his nature to engulf the whole skirt.

Because of this, I feel that a properly designed bait doesn't need a trailer hook. Trailer-hook believers will scoff at this, saying they've caught many fish with the trailer without the main hook being stuck. I don't doubt it, but this doesn't necessarily mean they would have missed the fish without the trailer. Any head-shaking fish stuck with two hooks will sometimes work one against the other, pulling one or both out. In any case, it's hard enough to set one large spinnerbait hook. Two hooks more than double the problem, and in many cases neither hook will be set properly, thereby missing a fish that might have been taken on a single hook. I say all this for the benefit of those anglers who have no opinion on a trailer hook, or who already question its use. Anglers dead set on using them will do so regardless of what I say here.

As a rule, trailer hooks are rigged with the point up, so that it rides behind and somewhat above the main hook. If I'm going to use one, I want it pointed the other way, an arrangement that gives much more bite. Anyone who goes after large pike or muskies with a spinnerbait ought to ponder the merits of these upside-down trailer hooks. Pike and muskies are easier to catch on trebles, and a large treble, or perhaps a double, can be used as a trailer hook.

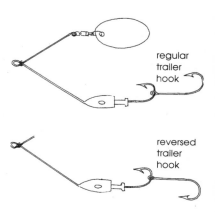

regular trailer hook

reversed trailer hook

One good reason for not using a trailer hook is that they make the bait more prone to collect weeds, a fact that nobody can deny. Another reason is that a trailer hook that flops around a lot is a constant pain in the neck. I saw a TV show the other day where the host was extolling the virtues of trailer hooks on one cast and explaining the need to tune the bait on the next. By tuning, he usually meant straightening out the trailer hook, and sometimes he fiddled a little with the wire. After almost every cast, the trailer hook (put on with surgical tubing, discussed later) was sticking out the side, and he "tuned" the bait, adjusting the trailer so that it was parallel with the main hook. Then he would go through the same routine on the next cast. What was happening, I think, is that the trailer hook flopped around when the lure splashed down at the end of the cast; after all, it would be the first thing to hit the water. If I'm right, the TV sport was "tuning" his bait for each *cast*, but not for the retrieve!

In any case, if you are going to use a trailer hook at all, you'll need one with a large eye, since it has to go over the barb of the main hook. Then it must be secured by a keeper of some sort, as discussed below.

Surgical Tubing. One of the best trailer-hook keepers is a short length of surgical tubing. The idea is to insert the eye of the trailer hook in the tubing; then insert the barb of the regular hook into the tubing, running it through the eye of the trailer hook and out the other side. Neat. If you've got good tubing with the right diameter, this method will also tend to hold the trailer hook straight behind the regular hook, where it ought to be. If the hook needs "tuning" frequently, it could be that a hole in the tube has wallowed out. So, replace the tube from time to time.

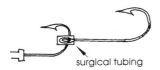
surgical tubing

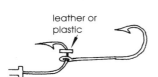
leather or plastic

Surgical tubing can be purchased in large rolls at some medical supply houses or, sometimes, from fishing-tackle outlets. Often, short lengths are packaged with trailer hooks. Remember also that the old-style slip-on skirts are made around a short piece of surgical tubing. Most of us have some old, matted skirts that can be torn up for the tubing. In a pinch, you can even rob a new slip-on skirt. You can use other kinds of tubing, such as the plastic tubing used for an aquarium air pump.

Leather or Plastic. Small pieces of leather can be used to hold the trailer hook on, or at least to keep it from slipping off. Neat ones can be made with the aid of a small punch, but a knife will also work, especially for those of square or triangular shape. Several kinds of plastic will work, but one of the best is the stuff used to hold 6-packs together. These can be picked up at any boat landing.

Vinyl. A neat keeper can be made by dipping the head of the trailer hook into the thick liquid plastic used for coating the handles of pliers or other tools. Of course, the dipping should be done long before the fishing trip. Dip a dozen or more hooks and let them dry. Then store them in a suitable container in your tackle box—or in your spinnerbait box in case you have half a dozen tackle boxes, as most of us do these days.

Anyway, this kind of skirt keeper works very well and will keep the trailer hook straight behind the regular hook, at least for a while. Once a hook starts to wear, it can be taken off and replaced by another one. The old ones can be reused by stripping off the plastic and dipping the eyes again.

Sharp Hooks

The advantages of sharp hooks should be self-evident, and I sometimes feel that I harp on the subject too much. The fact is that it's difficult to set a dull hook. The larger the hook and the larger the barb, the more difficult it is to set. A limber rod, a light line with lots of stretch, and long casts all contribute to missed strikes. Also, how the rod is held is important. For best results, point the rod toward the fish, so that it will have a wide strike arc. Anyone who holds a rod straight up in order to fish a buzzbait with a slower retrieve should know that he will miss some strikes.

In any case, the relatively large hooks used on spinnerbaits and buzzbaits, and on larger jigs, should be kept very sharp. In fact, some hooks should be sharpened before they are ever thrown into the water. There are all manner of hook-sharpening gadgets on the market, but I prefer a small, flat file. I might add that some of the new hooks with short points are difficult to resharpen.

A Good Point Isn't Enough. A good many stringers of fish are caught in barber shops across the land, and some lunkers are lost there, too. But not all of these reports are tall tales. Some really are true—but by default. Far too often, it doesn't take much of a fish to break or bend a hook.

Most hooks are manufactured from soft wire—almost noodle-soft. After the barb, the point, the eye, and the bend are formed in this soft wire, the hooks are then tempered and plated. Defective points, barbs, and eyes get past the shaping and machining process frequently enough, but these defects are relatively easy to spot. Imperfectly formed hooks are usually rejected before being used for fishing. The biggest problem and the hardest one to detect is in the tempering. For one reason or another, significant numbers of hooks fail to harden in the process—or don't get processed. Although they might look perfect even to the sharpest eye, they come out too soft. Softness, of course, is a matter of degree, but some rather large hooks, say 3/0, bend as easily as paper clips.

A spokesman for a large hook manufacturer admitted to me over the telephone that there was a problem. But he felt that the percentage of defects is small, and that the problem at his firm is no worse than at other mass manufacturers. In short, he wasn't too worried about it. Serious anglers will surely feel differently. *Any* defective hook put onto a lure, or into a package for sale, is one too many. A single hook can cause a fisherman to lose a trophy, sometimes after spending a good deal of time and money to have a chance to catch that trophy.

The bad thing, of course, is that after the tooling and plating processes, an improperly tempered hook looks exactly like the others and is almost impossible to detect. One spinnerbaitmaker of my acquaintance built a simple rig to test each hook by hand, but most of the larger luremakers play the percentage game in this highly competitive business. Zero defects costs money. Lots of money. It's up to the individual fisherman to test his hooks for temper, and the only good test is to try to bend the hook. Putting the point on the edge of a table and bending down by hand is one method. An ordinary pair of pliers will also work, and the knowledgeable angler should include a pair in the tackle box, along with hook files and hones.

Yes, it's true that a "soft" hook will often catch fish. If, for example, a deep-water bass swallows a plastic worm and is gut-hooked on a long or light line with a soft rod, it will likely end up in the boat. Under these circumstances, a bent paper clip might catch him. Tangling with the same fish in close quarters on a long, stiff, flipping rod with heavy no-stretch line might be another matter. If a hook bends in the fisherman's hands, it can also bend if the point hits a bone when it's set.

Soft hooks have no doubt been around for a long time, but it was only recently that the extent of the problem became clear to me. Hand-tied Living Rubber skirts on jigs, spinnerbaits, and buzzbaits brought the problem to light. In this process, a band of partly slit rubber about 1 inch wide is wrapped around the lure's skirt-keeper shank. Then the band is stretched back and the end is cut crosswise with scissors. When the rubber is stretched back to be cut, it applies a good deal of pressure on the hook, which is held in a heavy-duty fly-tying vise. If the hook is soft, it will bend. And brute strength is not all of the problem.

How much pressure is applied during the skirt-tying process depends on who is doing the work—and on the "tightness" of the rubber being used.

One custom lure manufacturer reported that an employee bent every hook in a batch of 25 dozen. That's 300 lures with bent hooks, all hidden by a thick Living Rubber skirt! So, remember to check your hook's configuration as well as its strength and sharpness.

Just as soft hooks have too little "temper," some have too much of a good thing and are too hard or too brittle. Although this problem isn't as common as soft hooks, it's still something to be reckoned with. Hard data or logical engineering explanations are unavailable, but in my limited experience the brittleness problem seems more common with cadmium-tin hooks than with nickel- or bronze-plated hooks. Sometimes these hooks break in the rounded bend, and jig hooks can break at the sharp 90-degree bend. Note that jig hooks can break at the bend *inside* the leadhead. I have seen dozens of 1-ounce jigs with loose hook eyelets that broke either when the mold was closed or when the lead was poured.

The brittleness problem seems more common with large hooks, but even small popping bugs should be inspected. In one case, the hook eye of a bluegill bug broke when I tightened down a clinch knot in a 6-pound tippet!

How bad is it? Detailed statistics are unavailable, but I've seen as many as 30 soft spinnerbait hooks (size 3/0) in a box of 1,000. Usually the percentage is closer to 3 hooks than to 30, but just 1 in 1,000 is too many. In recent years, the tempering of hooks seems to have become much more constant, but who knows what the future holds even for next year's batch. In any case, there are millions of old hooks still on the shelves and in tackle boxes.

I once sat in on a roundtable meeting between the late Lew Childre (who developed the speed-spool casting reels and was the first to put aluminum oxide rings on American rods), several of his executives, and a hook manufacturer. While inspecting some of the hooks, Lew surprised everybody by bringing out a pair of pliers and testing some in the bend. Quite a few gave under pressure, and he threw them out. Squirming, the hookmaker said that it was a new batch and that they would harden after a few months. Whether or not this is true is of no consequence here, but every angler ought to keep a pair of pliers in the tackle box, and use them on both new and old hooks. That, I say, is the ultimate test.

Spinner Blades

Most anglers who rely extensively on spinnerbaits like to have a wide choice of blades for one reason or another. Choice of color and finish often depends on the water, the time of day, the season of the year, and personal preference. I once knew two good anglers who fished with the same bass club in Florida. Both were what I call blade men, but one used only smooth Colorado blades—and he was perpetually frustrated because the local tackle shops stocked only hammered blades—while the other used only blades with "pimples," as he called hammered blades. Both caught plenty of fish.

The truth is that some blades will produce for one angler, but not necessarily for another. A good deal depends on how one fishes, the kind of spinnerbait, speed of retrieve, depth of lure, and so on. Perhaps the most important requirement is that the spinnerbait and its blades run true and feel right if the angler is to have the necessary confidence to catch bass consistently. The plain truth is that confidence in lure and tackle is essential to becoming an outstanding angler.

Choice of blade should depend largely on how the angler wants the blade to swing. A Colorado blade swings wide, an Indiana blade swings tighter, and a willowleaf blade revolves close to the shaft's axis without much swing at all. Thus, willowleaf blades, which have been popular in parts of Louisiana for many years, tend to work better in grass and vegetation. Colorado blades revolve slower but offer more water resistance, and thus produce a more pronounced throb per blade revolution. Colorado blades, rigged in tandem, tend to work better, or at least they're more popular, for fishing open, shallow water. Indiana blades fit somewhere between the two, and some people prefer the Indiana shape for fishing deep.

Ironically, a tandem-blade spinnerbait will usually take a larger rear blade than will a single-spin. Maybe the front blade of a tandem-spin turns one way and the rear blade turns the other, producing countertorque. For

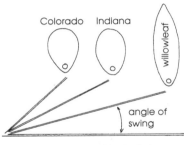

Comparative Blade Swing

this reason, tandem-spins are often used for baits meant to be fished just under the surface, producing a burbling wake.

The blade color—painted, copper, nickel, etc.—doesn't have much to do with throb and feel, other things being equal. But other things are not equal. Not by a long shot. There is a vast difference between the weight of spinner blades of the same size and shape. Some size 4 Colorado blades, for example, weigh almost twice as much as others of identical size and contour. Why? Because of the base material from which they are made. In fact, the unit weight and the thickness of the material are, or should be, important considerations. Steel blades tend to be cheaper than brass. They also tend to be thinner and lighter. Because they are lighter, they don't produce the same throb or vibrations when they're pulled through the water. As a rule of thumb, the heavier the blade, the heavier the throb.

Base material and finish also have a lot to do with how expensive a blade is, and do-it-yourselfers who purchase components for spinnerbaits know that a lacquered, hammered-copper blade costs twice as much as some hammered, nickel-plated blades. Why? Top-quality copper blades are made from a brass blank. The brass is plated with copper, then the blade is coated with lacquer to help keep it from tarnishing. Some of the nickel blades are made by thinly plating steel blanks, with no lacquer coatings. Thus, the top-line copper blade will not only be twice as expensive but will also be heavier compared with some cheap nickel blades. It will also have a different throb when retrieved at normal speed.

Consciously or unconsciously, blade throb is more important to most fishermen than blade expense. (Lure manufacturers may pinch pennies, but most anglers don't.) Some anglers who show a marked preference for copper blades may like the action more than the color, although they might not realize it. Anyone who doubts the relation between throb and weight should put a light plastic blade on a spinnerbait, cast it out, and retrieve it as usual; then repeat the procedure with a lacquered copper Colorado blade of the same size.

In addition to weight, the topics below should be considered when rigging or choosing a spinnerbait.

BLADE SHAPES AND SIZES

Size and shape have a good deal to do with how much throb or vibration a spinner blade makes. The larger the blade, the heavier the throb. Because a blade also produces torque, however, there is a practical limit on blade size. A size 8 (silver-dollar-size) Colorado blade attached to a ¼-ounce spinnerbait won't ride straight up as it ought to. A ⅛-ounce bait rigged with a number 8 blade might even ride upside down. Speed of retrieve is also a factor. A ⅜-ounce bait might carry a number 8 blade on a slow retrieve, but will surely tilt at burbling speed.

Colorado Blades. Although willowleaf blades came on strong for a while, the Colorado blade is, year in and year out, the most popular among bass anglers. Except during fads, it is the blade used most often by manufacturers. It swings wide and makes a good throb, which is very important to some anglers. In short, it is an easy blade to feel, and that characteristic has no doubt contributed to its popularity over the years.

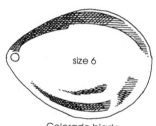

size 6

Colorado blade

As a rule, a Colorado blade is the choice for fishing in shallow water. Since it swings wide and creates a lot of water resistance, it tends to run shallow. Of course, this feature makes it ideal for burbling the surface. Other blades will burble, but the Colorado does it on a slower retrieve. The Colorado is also the preferred blade for fishing a single-spin as a fall bait.

Colorado blades come in 11 or 12 sizes, as follows: 00, 0, 1, 1½, 2, 3, 3½, 4, 4½, 5, 6, 7, and 8. Other sizes may be added from time to time, and not all manufacturers or suppliers make or stock all sizes. (Also, a new "Magnum" blade is available from Lakeland Industries.) One big problem is that the sizes vary from one manufacturer to another. A number 5 Colorado from Worth Company is close to a number 6 Colorado from Lakeland, for example.

Although the smaller jig-spinner attachments use tiny Colorado blades, most of the spinnerbaits are rigged with blades from size 3 to 6, but bigger blades are sometimes used. One of my favorite baits for catching bass is a ⅝-ounce frog-head bait with a size 7 front blade and a size 8 rear blade. But this thing will wear you out during a hard day's fishing, and it doesn't cast well with light tackle.

A good many people who rig their own baits, or who custom-rig for other anglers, put large blades on a light bait. The trouble with such blade-heavy baits is that they tend to lean to one side or the other on the retrieve. The faster the retrieve, the more they lean. Anglers who know their blades understand this, and will fish the lure slowly, at least until they're ready to snake it on in and make another cast.

If I design the head and the wire, I can rig a tandem-spin that runs straight up at all speeds—or at least at speeds I can attain by cranking fast. To accomplish this on a ⅜-ounce bait with Colorado blades, for example, I would choose a size 4 rear blade and a 3½ front blade, spaced with four ⅛-ounce beads. With a ¼-ounce lure, I would go down to a 3½ on the rear and a 3 up front. Of course, smaller blades could also be used, but larger blades tend to upset the balance. The goal, it seems to me, is to rig with baits that run well with the largest possible blades at normal fishing speeds. Of course, how you intend to fish a spinnerbait has a bearing on how it should be rigged. Small blades sink faster and run deeper—and they tend to run straight without constant tuning. Large blades make the lure ride on top, but they often present tuning problems.

Single-spins are always more difficult to tune than tandem-spins, and the choice of the single blade is more critical. Anyone who is slow rolling a spinnerbait in deep water (or using it as a fall bait) isn't much interested in how well the bait tracks on a fast retrieve. He wants a blade that produces maximum throb, and, of course, the larger the blade the more water resistance, other things being equal.

striped Indiana blade

Indiana. Although some well-known lures are rigged with Indiana blades, this shape has never gained much favor with bass anglers as a group. Since they tend to run deeper, they're generally considered to be walleye blades—or they have been in the past. But things change, and, in some areas, Indiana blades are certainly popular even for bass. As a rule, they aren't available in quite so many sizes as Colorado blades, and usually the half-sizes are missing entirely.

Indiana blades work nicely on jig spinners, although they're seldom used for that purpose, at least not by the major manufacturers. They're rarely chosen by anglers who want a bait for buzzing the surface, or for fishing on the fall; they'll work, but they aren't ideal. I feel they're good blades for ordinary cast-and-crank fishing (which covers about 90 percent of it), but not for special applications.

In the main, the comments about the sizes for rigging Colorado blades will apply to Indiana blades, but up the sizes by 1. In other words, a size 4 Colorado blade has about as much surface area as a size 5 Indiana blade. It's not quite the same, but it's close enough.

Idaho Blades. These blades, marketed by Hilderbrandt, are almost exactly the same as Colorado blades.

Willowleaf Blades. A few years ago, willowleaf blades suddenly got very hot and were in great demand in tackle shops. I forget exactly what started the fad, and it probably doesn't matter. In any case, willowleaf blades swing almost around their own axis, which makes them ideal for going through grass; they've been popular in Louisiana and other grassy areas for many years.

Heretofore, willowleaf blades were on the small side. What got hot were very large willowleafs—so large that they stuck out far behind the skirt. That's what people wanted, and some local machine-shop owners suddenly got into the spinner-blade business. In any case, these large blades will catch lots of bass—big bass—and I think they have more flash than a Colorado or an Indiana blade. Since the blade tends to turn tightly around its own axis, the fish sees more of it. Think about it. Rig several baits and throw them into a swimming pool. Notice that the Colorado swings wide in a blur. If the blade swings at 45 degrees, that would be the most likely angle for a bass to approach the bait. If so, wouldn't it see the blade edgewise for the most part? From the same angle, a large willowleaf would stream back, and be highly visible. What all this boils down to is that willowleafs have more flash but less throb compared with a Colorado blade with the same surface area.

At first, the trend was to use large willowleaf blades on the rear of a tandem-spin, following a surprisingly small Colorado up front. This led to

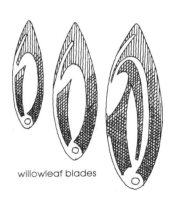

willowleaf blades

other combinations, and it's not unusual these days to see two willowleafs rigged on the same bait. For some reason, willowleaf blades are seldom used as single-spins, partly, I suppose, because single-spins usually have shorter arms, and the blade might get in the way when the hook is set. In my opinion, none of the spinnerbaits on the market are ideal for use with large willowleaf blades. My ideas on this matter are in Chapter 2.

Willowleaf blades come in several sizes, from a number 1, which is about ¾ inch long, to a number 8, which is about 4 inches long. There is also considerable variation in blade size among manufacturers, so that one company's size 5 might be another's 4½. I recommend rigging tandem-spins with ⅜-ounce heads with a size 3 Colorado and a size 4½ or 5 willowleaf, although a size 2 Colorado and a size 7 or even 8 willowleaf are sometimes used. The big blades will certainly catch bass, but they don't cast as nicely as a more reasonable size and, as the old joke goes, spinnerbaits rigged with large willowleafs look like helicopters during the cast. For a ¼-ounce bait, a size 5 willowleaf blade is pushing it; I don't think this size handles larger blades too well. But a ¼-ounce long-armed head, rigged with a size 2 Colorado blade and a size 4 willowleaf makes an ideal bait for fishing grassy waters. The blade goes through the grass easier, and the relatively light head also helps keep the bait out of trouble. As a grass bait, I prefer a single-spin with a long arm and an extra kick in the bend, as shown in the drawing. This helps the grass and silt ride over the top of the swivel, which, if clogged, can keep the blade from turning.

extra bend in end of wire
helps keep silt out of swivel
on this weed bait

A willowleaf blade can be used as a skitter blade, in which case it should be rigged without a swivel by simply inserting the blade directly into the wire loop with the cupped side riding up. I've never seen a bait rigged this way, except tied onto my own fishing rod, but surely someone must have done it. Since I sometimes fish with a fast retrieve, I am fond of this rig in rather shallow water (5 or 6 feet), and I find it very effective at times. But the consensus is that slowly fished lures take more bass, and I won't argue about it.

I said earlier that I don't know where the large willowleaf blade fad got started, but I think it was popularized by Roland Martin, who used the bait on Lake Okeechobee—ideal for this bait since it is relatively shallow, has lots of grass, and is full of both large golden shiners and big bass. Golden shiners are nest robbers, and big bass have to fight them continuously while they're on the bed. I think bass hate golden shiners and will hit them at every opportunity, whether they're hungry or not. Since large willowleaf blades seem to reflect more light than Colorado blades, I use gold blades in waters that hold golden shiners. In large impoundments filled with shad, silver might work better.

In any case, willowleaf blades are available in a variety of surface finishes, including some that are highly polished in a concentric circle pattern and others with a prismatic finish. Painted blades are also popular in some areas, especially in sizes 3 through 5. White and chartreuse are the most popular colors.

A new "magnum willow blade," said to be good for pike and muskie, has recently come onto the market. It's not really a willowleaf blade, being more of a diamond shape, but it will catch fish. It is available in sizes 6 and 7.

Ripple and Swing Blades. These blades are long and slender like willowleafs, but are a little more rounded on the ends. Typically, they are used on such in-line baits as the Shyster and the Rooster Tail, usually in the smaller sizes, from ¼ ounce on down. Like the willowleafs, these blades have a narrow swing and produce more flash than a Colorado or Indiana blade. For this reason, they're suggestive of some minnows, and baits rigged with them are very productive, on a slow retrieve, for crappie, white bass, and other fish that feed extensively on minnows. Although I once caught three bass larger than 8 pounds within 15 minutes with a Super Rooster Tail rigged with such a blade, they aren't commonly used for bass fishing. In general, these blades aren't available in a wide range of sizes and finishes; swing blades are usually smooth or textured, and ripple blades have slanted ribs.

Sonic and French Blades. These neat blades, commonly used on in-line baits like the Mepps, are available in several finishes and sizes, from small to medium. The idea is that the recessed or cupped blade creates a fish-calling sonic effect. In any case, they catch fish, and I have rigged them quite successfully on regular spinnerbaits. Often these blades are painted, sometimes with dots or other geometric patterns.

Presto Blades. These interesting blades are available, at present, in only two sizes: large and small. The finishes are also rather limited, but both nickel and gold are available. They are flat blades, without a cup, but have a pronounced lip at the end. They turn freely, and I love to fish them on smaller spinnerbaits, and as tandem-spins on in-line baits. I usually rig these only on ¼-ounce tandem-spin baits, although I have fished them on ⅛-ounce single-spins. I also like them on jig spinners for ¼- and ⅛-ounce heads.

In-Line Blades. These blades, available in several types, are designed to swing freely around a shaft without the aid of a clevis. They are used almost exclusively on in-line spinnerbaits or buzzbaits, and are discussed in Chapter 7.

Doc Shelton Trolls. I don't know the history of these blades, but they're sometimes rigged on spinnerbaits. They're available in sizes 3 through 8, and in several finishes.

MIXING BLADES

A willowleaf rear blade and a Colorado front blade seem like a natural combination, but of course anglers and manufacturers looking for something new put all manner of blades together, in all finishes. Some people want hammered copper on the rear and hammered nickel on the front, or vice versa. Or perhaps smooth nickel willowleaf on the rear and a hammered brass Colorado on the front. I've seen times when anglers would fish with nothing but a particular

ripple blade

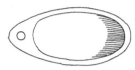

swing blades

2   3   5

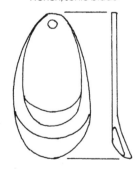

French/sonic blade

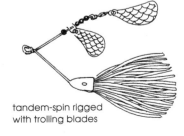

presto blades

tandem-spin rigged
with trolling blades

combination. By the time the local tackle shop stocked up with these, something else got hot. You'd almost suspect somebody was manipulating the market here and there, with the aid of hero-and-hawg tournament pros and TV personalities, but, on the other hand, most bass anglers are absolute suckers for something new. My suggestion is to join right in and create your own fads, with, of course, some outlandish combination that no other angler has. If you fish competitively, it's always good to tie on a lure rigged with some new combination, saying to your partner, "I hope they don't start hitting this. It's the only one I've got." All's fair in love, war, and bass fishing.

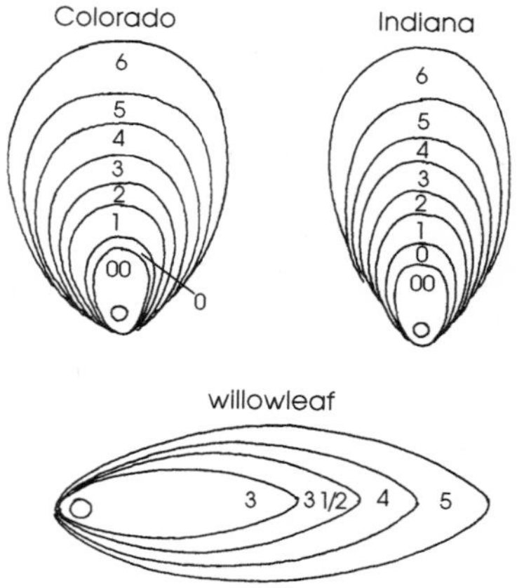

MATCHING BLADE SIZE TO HEAD WEIGHT

Now we come to more serious ground. If the blade isn't pretty well matched to the head, the lure won't run straight. Trial and error is the only true test, and variation in head and wire design also come into play. As stated in Chapter 2, the wire's length and angle determine how well the bait balances. The tables below are fairly safe recommendations, but of course experts will make the blades larger or smaller, depending on how they fish or what they want to do. An angler who fishes a ¼-ounce single-spin rather fast might have to use a size 3½ blade, but the angler who fishes slow can use a size 4 or even 4½.

Comparative Sizes of Spinner Blades

SINGLE-SPINS

Head Size	Kind of Blade		
	Colorado	Indiana	Willowleaf
⅛	2½	3	3½
¼	3	4	4
⅜	4	5	4½
½	5	6	5
¾	6	7	6 or 7

DOUBLE-SPINS

Head Size	Kind of Blade		
	Colorado	Indiana	Willowleaf
⅛	1-2	2-3	1-3½
¼	3-3½	3-4	2-4
⅜	3½-4½	4-5	3-4½
½	4-5	5-6	3½-5
¾	5-6	6-7	3½-6 or 7

*Small Colorado in front; willowleaf in rear.

BLADE SURFACE FINISH

The blade's surface finish, usually hammered or smooth, is largely a matter of personal preference, although there are subtle differences.

Hammered Blades. These have more water resistance compared with a smooth blade of similar shape and size. They also reflect light differently, reflecting a thousand tiny points instead of a continuous flash. These blades aren't formed and then hammered, as might be implied, but are cut, or stamped, from an embossed sheet of metal.

Some blades have a similar finish, and are made the same way. But the pattern is different from ordinary hammered blades, and is intended to resemble fish scales.

Smooth Blades. These slick blades go through the water with a little less resistance than hammered blades, but if there's a difference in "throb," it's quite small. Smooth blades reflect light more like a mirror than hammered blades do.

Fluted and Ribbed. These blades have a little more water resistance than do smooth blades, and may create a different sort of turbulence in the water. If these attract more bass, the evidence isn't clear to me. In any case, the flutes or ribs are shaped into the metal, and are more than a mere surface finish.

fluted blades

ribbed blades

THE CUP

Although blade finish is important to some anglers, the matter of cup is more fundamental to what the blade is designed to do. Most blades are concave/convex, like a tablespoon. This helps them spin in the water, and influences the vibrations the blade sends out. Some people believe that the deeper the cup, the better the vibes, but I have no evidence to support this. Nevertheless, I like a blade with a good cup, but I feel that the normal blade shape, which has evolved over the years, is perhaps the best design.

Some so-called deep-cupped blades have a convex/concave shape, with a sort of kicker lip at the end. These work nicely and seem to turn better on a slow retrieve. I like them.

As a rule, the cup starts at the outer edge of the blade, as on Colorado, Indiana, and willowleaf blades. Sonic or French blades are different, however, in that the cup starts in from the end a ways, leaving a flat area all around the edge. These work well, and millions of them have been used on the Mepps and other lures. They are popular on in-line spinnerbaits and are not normally available in cow-bell sizes.

Other blades, such as the presto, are rather flat and have a cupped lip at the end. Do-it-yourselfers can sometimes put a lip in some other blades with pliers, and I have even put a slight spiral in willowleaf blades to make them work at a very slow retrieve. Other modifications can be made. For instance, brass blades can be worked down with a ball-peen hammer or a similar tool.

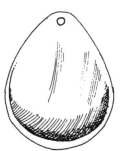

deep-cup blades
have an extra lip
in the end

BLADE MATERIAL AND FINISH

As discussed elsewhere in this chapter, a blade's weight depends on the base metal and its thickness, and on the plating and painting. Spinnerbaitmakers have a variety of finishes to choose from, especially for the more popular Colorado, Indiana, and willowleaf blades.

Nickel. These blades are probably more popular than any other finish, for several reasons: the flash is good, the blade is inexpensive, and nickel doesn't tarnish easily. At one time, nickel was coated onto unpolished brass blades by an electroplating process. In recent years, nickel has also been coated onto steel blades, which are cheaper and lighter.

All nickel blades are highly polished; the finish is available in smooth and hammered surfaces.

Copper. These blades are much more expensive than those plated with nickel, but they usually are made pretty much the same way in either hammered or smooth finish. The big problem is that copper tarnishes quickly, and the blades must be coated with lacquer. As a rule, copper blades are much heavier than nickel, although there are differences among brands. Anglers like copper, and some people use copper in dark water and nickel in clear water; others reverse this rule of thumb.

Brass. Widely available in all popular blade shapes, brass makes an inexpensive blade because it doesn't require coating. It will take a high polish, but some component suppliers also stock unpolished blades as well. For the best results, brass blades should be lacquered.

I know one fellow, who dabbled for a while in commercial luremaking, who wouldn't use brass blades because they were the cheapest that money could buy. Most large manufacturers, however, think the other way. In any case, brass blades are simply not very popular with bass anglers in most areas.

Two-toned Blades. It's true. You can buy blades that are nickel on the convex side and copper on the concave side. I have used these, but I don't see any advantage.

Silver. I was trying to finagle a loan with my banker one day when a fellow crashed the meeting with an announcement that the price of silver had dropped. With the banker's backing, this fellow had built up a printing business from scratch, and had recently sold it for several million dollars (at least that's the figure that was rumored in these parts). Since the banker had financed his original business venture, the printer had turned to him for advice in investing his fortune. The banker had made several suggestions, saying that gold might be a good way to go with part of the cash.

The printer jumped right onto precious metals, saying that silver might be better since it was used in the printing business and would always be in great demand. He bought heavily in silver futures in the neighborhood of $19 an ounce, if I remember correctly. Eventually, silver started dropping—and it had taken another plunge the day before he barged into my meeting.

"Oh? How low is it?" the banker asked.

"It's under $12," the printer said.

"Good lord," said the banker. "If it's that cheap, buy some more."

I don't know whether he bought some more, but the price of silver is now about $7 an ounce. In any case, fluctuations in silver prices had an influence on the history of spinner blades. A very large lure company once put out an in-line bait with silver blades, claiming that they had a different reflection in the water and cast light in such a manner that it attracted more fish. At the time, they were the only firm with a silver-plated blade, and I had to buy the whole in-line lure just to get a blade for a doglegged single-spin. I'm not a fish but I spent a good deal of time looking at silver versus nickel blades in the relatively clear waters of Lake Weir in Florida. (I wasn't *fishing*, you understand, but was working hard at lure research.) I never did determine which finish the local bass really preferred, but I did come to the conclusion that there was a difference between silver and nickel to the human eye.

At a certain point, the lure company quit using silver blades and dropped the sales pitch, apparently being more interested in cutting costs than in attracting fish. Now that silver has come down to a reasonable price, Lakeland (and perhaps other manufacturers) offer a new line of silver-plated blades. (Some manufacturers will do custom plating.) Stock items now include silver-plated blades in all sizes of Colorado, Indiana, and willowleaf shapes, as well as presto and perhaps a few others.

Gold Blades. These are now stocked by some of the large suppliers, but not many years ago they were plated on an as-ordered basis, and the price varied daily, with the market. This stopped a lot of manufacturers from using gold in spite of the fact that, along the Gulf Coast, gold-plated blades are almost necessary to sell a spinnerbait.

Of course, gold-plated blades are still expensive, but the price has pretty much stabilized in recent years. They are available in hammered and smooth finishes in most popular sizes and shapes. I like them on very large willowleaf blades in Florida, where large golden shiners catch large bass.

Black Nickel. This metallic finish is available on Colorado, Indiana, and willowleaf blades. In the water it has a grayish cast; it may be the least visible of all the metallic or painted finishes. It's a good choice for those anglers, and I am one, who don't want to call attention to their blades. I could be wrong on this point, however. The best you can do is rig with black nickel blades and look at them in the water. Then hope that the fish see them the same way that you do.

Painted Blades. At one time, painted blades tended to flake or chip, and they were often sprayed with a chalky feeling chartreuse, or orange, or other color. These days, at least some manufacturers use slicker paints, and these tend to hold up better. My thinking may be warped on this subject, however, because I've had thousands of blades get chipped in bulk bags during transport. Thousands.

In any case, all sizes of painted Colorado, Indiana, and willowleaf blades are readily available as stock items. Hagen's, for example, lists the following solid colors: red, blue, orange, green, chartreuse, black, purple, white, yellow, and pink.

In addition to solid colors, we also have a wide choice of striped blades. These are interesting to see in action in the water, and if I wanted to call attention to a blade I would probably choose one of these, such as black and yellow. In fact, I am fond of fishing an in-line bait with a chartreuse-and-black striped blade, and a chartreuse-and-black skirt. With in-line baits, the blade can indeed become part of the lure, but, as I've said more than once, it may be a mistake to call attention to blades on top-riding spinnerbaits; those "blade nipper" bass might well miss the hook. Striped blades were probably a spin-off from the highly successful striped wobble spoons; with them, the angler would indeed want the fish to be attracted to the blade. Striped blades are available in several color combinations, and custom colors are also available.

scale finish   diamond finish

In addition to stripes, blades are often decorated with other color schemes. A black blade with yellow spots, for example, is sometimes used on in-line baits, but, again, I don't recommend them for top-riding spinner blades. Some of these blades have round dots, and others have diamonds. Still others have a fish-scale pattern.

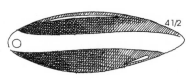

striped finish

Some of the neatest blades I've seen were painted with Imron (a tough polyurethane paint used on trucks and boats), exactly the color of the spinnerbait head. I am especially fond of silver with metalflake and gold with metalflake. Also, some blades can be dipped in vinyl paint, but in some cases the blade's finish may prevent the paint from sticking properly. Plain steel blades can be painted successfully with Imron, but these are difficult to find, and I'd recommend that hobbyists experiment with plain (unpolished) brass. Any polished blade should probably be roughed up with emery cloth before painting.

Prismatic Blades. These blades are used on some of the Strike King baits and have been in great demand from time to time by anglers who want the fish to see the blades or who are following the latest trend. Similar blades are sometimes marketed as components, so that the do-it-yourselfer doesn't necessarily have to purchase a whole bait just to get the blade. Also remember that stick-on prismatic tape can be stuck onto spinner blades.

Pearl Blades. These blades, made from natural mussel shells, are very pretty in the water and out; they're usually available in only a few small sizes of Indiana blades. Although pearl blades will catch lots of fish and work well on trolling rigs, they're too fragile for casting into stumps and aren't available in sizes large enough for most safety-pin spinnerbaits. Anyone interested in pearl blades ought to experiment with some of the new pearlescent lure paints.

PLASTIC BLADES

At one time, clear plastic blades made something of a splash, and the magazines plugged them as being deadly in clear water. Other colors were also available, with or without metalflake. The first ones I saw were concave on one side and flat on the other; a new line featured a Colorado shape with convex/concave sides.

I've caught fish with plastic blades, but they simply don't have the mass of metal blades and don't make the same vibes, although one brand was called "Good Vibes." In any case, they simply don't have the right throb for spinnerbaits, in my opinion.

MODIFIED BLADES

I have known lure manufacturers to drill holes in spinner blades or otherwise modify them just for the sake of doing something new. A spokesman for one large lure company said that holes in the blades helped sales, but he admitted that he didn't really know whether or not they caught more fish.

I don't put much stock in most such gimmicks, but I do think that the blade's weight in relation to its surface area makes a difference. As stated earlier in this chapter, a heavy blade makes a better throb (within limits). Tackle tinkerers might want to consider sticking two thin blades together. Solder isn't necessary. Some of the autobody-repair bonding agents and fillers work fine, and some vinyl paints or fly-tying head cements also work nicely, at least for a while, as do water-resistant super glues such as Zap-a-Gap.

Clamping or otherwise holding the blades together under pressure helps. Most any sort of clamp works fine, including Vise-Grip pliers. Blades of different colors can be joined, or even blades of different sizes. (Usually, it isn't advisable to try to match up the holes in blades of different sizes; instead, work with the center of the blades, matching the curvatures.) But don't stick too many spinner blades together, especially in the larger sizes. Too much weight will make your spinnerbait top heavy and cause it to run upside down.

Believe it or not, I once knew an angler who made his own spinner blades by hammering coins to shape. He even used an elongated and cupped silver dollar successfully on a ¾-ounce head.

THE BOTTOM LINE

Counting the various shapes, sizes, finishes, and thicknesses, well over 4,000 different spinner blades are available. Such a selection can be perplexing to the luremakers and tackle-shop owners who have to worry about keeping the newfangled lures in supply, but the tackle tinkerer never had it so good.

If your primary interest is catching fish, it's best to keep your head clear and remember that the key to choosing a blade for a successful spinnerbait has more to do with vibration than with flash. Consciously or unconsciously, a properly rigged spinnerbait makes a throb that is transmitted up the line, along the rod, and into the angler's hand. In short, the blade keeps the angler in touch with the lure. This is extremely important—and it's part of why some bass anglers will pay extra for a sensitive graphite rod. My recommendation is to play around with colors and finishes and sizes and shapes if it pleases you to do so—but get real serious when you close your eyes and feel for the spinnerbait's throb.

Rigging
Spinnerbaits

Chapter

5

The mechanics of rigging spinnerbaits are simple enough. The hardest part is forming a small loop in the end of the wire, and selecting the right hardware. Blades were discussed in the previous chapter, and the text below lists all the various beads, swivels, clevises, and so on that are readily available at this writing. New products come along from time to time—including a few true improvements.

My thinking on rigging spinnerbaits is that the components (except for the blade) should be as small as possible, within limits. Why? Two reasons. First, I don't want to call the fish's attention to the rigging instead of to the skirt and hook. Second, larger components add more weight to the top riding arm and also add more water resistance. The weight should be at the hook, not at the top, so that the bait will track straight.

SINGLE-SPINS

Some people put beads on a single-spin wire, but I've never known why. All you need do is make a loop, insert the swivel, close the loop, and attach a blade. The loop can be formed with needlenose pliers, but these make a loop that isn't round. Special round, tapered needlenose pliers are available, and they work very well. Note that the size of the loop can be determined by the position of the taper and point of contact. The best bet is to make yourself what I call a looper. This is a special hand-held tool made using two posts with a gap between them. There are many ways to accomplish this, but my nephew David Livingston came up with a way to make them fairly quickly. First, he turns down the end of a nail, then he wraps it with fine copper wire parallel to another nail. Then he molds lead around this unit, making a neat hand-held, two-prong "looper." Insert the wire between the two prongs, and turn the handle with the right hand while holding the wire firmly in the left hand. In a second you have a perfect loop. More elaborate bending tools are discussed in Chapter 12, but I consider

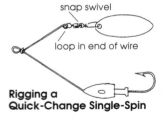

snap swivel

loop in end of wire

**Rigging a
Quick-Change Single-Spin**

forming a simple loop to be part of rigging the bait, and that it is best accomplished with a hand-held tool.

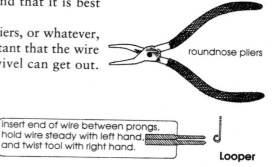

roundnose pliers

insert end of wire between prongs, hold wire steady with left hand, and twist tool with right hand.

Looper

After you've formed the loop, either with a looper, pliers, or whatever, insert the end of the swivel and close the loop. It's important that the wire loop be closed all the way down; if a gap is left, the swivel can get out. Some people force the end of the wire on past the arm and leave it there, creating a snag on which to hang silt. It's okay to force the end down, but adjust it so that the wire is butted together and centered.

I like a fairly small loop, which makes a stronger connection and is easier to close down. If it's too small, however, it may foul the swivel, cocking it off to one side so that the bait doesn't run straight. For closing the loop, I highly recommend the large split-ring pliers from Lakeland Industries. These have holes in the jaws, or matching semicircular slots in each jaw, that hold the loop in place while it is squeezed shut. Perfect. These pliers are available from some of the distributors and suppliers. They aren't as cheap as some split-ring pliers, but are worth the price.

TANDEM-SPINS

All of the above comments about attaching a swivel to the end of a single-spin wire apply to tandem-spins. Before the loop is formed in the wire, the front blade, clevis, and spacers must be added, strung up as shown in the illustration.

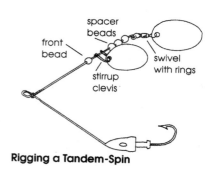

spacer beads

front bead

swivel with rings

stirrup clevis

Rigging a Tandem-Spin

Start the rigging with a small bead slid onto the wire arm. (The bead keeps silt and debris out of the clevis.) Next, hook the clevis through the blade and insert the ends of the clevis through both holes. Add three beads or a spacer of some sort; these separate the front blade from the rear blade. I like to have at least 5/32 of an inch between blades, which takes three 1/8-inch beads. There's a surprisingly wide choice of spacers, and sometimes sleeves are used instead of bends.

SWIVELS AND CONNECTORS

Swivels make a free-wheeling connection between the spinner blade and the wire. Some swivels work better than others, depending in part on the design and in part on how well the individual parts are made and how they're put together. In other words, there can be lemons in the best of designs. There isn't a standard test for a swivel, but what I call the flick test is reliable and much practiced by spinnerbait sharps. The idea is to rig a blade on a swivel, hold the swivel so that the blade hangs straight down, and flick the edge of the blade, setting it in motion. How long the blade turns is an indication of the swivel's quality, and is roughly related to how well the blade will turn on a slow retrieve. Having a swivel, blade, and lure combination that works perfectly is very important to expert anglers who fish the single-spin as a fall bait in deep water. The swivel isn't so important when the spinnerbait is merely cast out and reeled in at a normal rate of retrieve. I call this cast-and-crank fishing, and I am fond of doing it when I'm angry at New York editors.

Another requirement is that the swivel and its connectors must hold the spinner blade. Don't laugh. Think about this. When casting, the angler jerks the rod back and then jerks it forward; the bait must in turn stop abruptly and start forward, which is where the blade slings off. Large blades sometimes open up the snaps and even strip split rings. That's right. Some of the imported ball-bearing swivels are rigged with very soft split rings, and even some of the more expensive rings aren't tempered properly. If you have swivels with sorry rings, it's best to put a drop of solder on them if you fish with large blades. Several kinds of connectors are used on swivels, and these will be discussed below before we get to the main component.

Connectors

ball-bearing swivel with split rings

Split Rings. These are often used to connect blades to the swivel, and, in the case of ball-bearing swivels, they're also used to connect the swivel to the wire. As indicated above, avoid sorry rings. Most of the stainless steel rings are adequate, and I like the so-called German rings, which are nickel-plated tempered steel. Rings are available in several sizes; the smaller sizes are best for rigging spinnerbaits.

Split rings can be put on with the aid of split-ring pliers. These spread the wire open so that the ring can be started through the blade, then the pliers are sort of wiggled several times, turning the ring 360 degrees. This is difficult to explain, and, no matter how I describe it, you'll need practice to develop speed with this tool. I've had practice. Some split-ring pliers aren't as good as others, and some work satisfactorily only with larger rings. Although I recommend buying a good pair of split-ring pliers (which look like needlenose pliers with a protruding lip on the end), I seldom use them to put a blade onto a ball-bearing swivel that has factory-attached rings. The trick here is to pinch the ring between your fingers so that the opening is on top. Turn the blade sideways and insert it between the wire, turning when you get the hole and the end of the wire lined up. Then hold the ring while working the blade by steps around it. This is harder to describe than to do.

inexpensive split-ring pliers

Purists want to use split rings instead of snaps on spinnerbaits, and I agree that they work a little better and are smaller and neater. The disadvantage is that changing from one blade to another is harder than it is with a snap. It's really easier to change spinnerbaits. I've seen TV footage, either ads or live action—and it's sometimes hard to tell which is which—where the host changed blades by changing the whole swivel and blade assembly. This was accomplished by opening up the wire, inserting a new swivel and blade assembly, and closing up the wire loop.

In any case, I am a firm believer in good split rings, and I recommend that any angler get a supply for rigging spinnerbaits and other purposes. They can be used to attach hooks to lures, or to attach the line to a lure eyelet, thereby giving the lure more action. I highly recommend the German steel rings, if you can find them, but I have seen soft ones mixed in with the good ones. Like soft hooks, they somehow got by without any tempering at all.

Safety-Pin Snaps. These snaps are usually satisfactory for holding a spinner blade, but they must be of top quality. Some of them are too soft, are manufactured improperly, or both. Frankly, I don't recommend these snaps for spinner blades—and certainly not for attaching a lure or hook to a line. Normally, these snaps are rigged onto the swivels at the factory so that no intermediate link is needed. As a rule, safety-pin snaps are suitable for small blades, such as those used on jig spinners, but I don't use them for large blades.

Interlock Snaps. These snaps are inherently stronger than safety-pin snaps, and the smaller sizes are certainly suitable for spinnerbaits. When used on spinnerbaits, they're usually attached to the swivel during manufacture. In other words, the bait is rigged with a snap swivel. I prefer the smaller sizes, always.

Coastlock Snaps. This design has a rather long snap mechanism and is not normally used on spinnerbaits.

Duo-Snaps. I love these snaps, if they're made of good-quality steel. Since they can be opened on both ends, they can be easily attached to swivels, although they don't fit the post in ball-bearing swivels without a little finagling. I like the smaller size for spinnerbaits.

Eyelock Snaps. The first time I saw these snaps, they were marketed by R-J Tackle (at one time called Ric-Jig) under the name Sock-eye snaps. Apparently R-J got out of the bulk components business, but now a similar snap is being marketed by Rosco. They are very easy to use, and the smaller sizes work well with spinnerbaits. My only objection is that they, like Coastlock snaps, are a little too long for my taste.

So much for connections. Now to the main component. Several kinds of swivels can be used on spinnerbaits, and some are quite expensive compared with the rest of the bait; some are quite inexpensive.

Swivels

Ball-Bearing Swivels. In recent years, much emphasis has been put on using ball-bearing swivels on spinnerbaits. While I agree in principle, I'll have to say that some crane swivels are much better than some ball-bearing swivels; further, ball-bearing swivels simply aren't needed for some kinds of fishing.

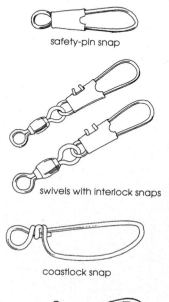

safety-pin snap

swivels with interlock snaps

coastlock snap

Duo-lock snap

eyelock snap

The truth is that some ball-bearing swivels don't spin properly; some don't spin at all. If anyone doubts this, I'd like to sell them a 25-gross bag of some size 2's that were made in the Orient. I'll sell cheap.

Even the most expensive of ball-bearing swivels have defects. In general, the quality seems to depend largely on the quality of the ball bearings themselves. These should be uniform and round. Further, all the ball bearings should be seated in the race so that the swivel post doesn't bind and prevent the blade from turning freely. Because a good deal depends on the quality of the ball bearings, there is some difference in individual swivels in a generally good batch. That's why so many expert blade men spend a lot of time flicking the blade and watching it revolve.

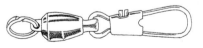

Sampo ball-bearing swivel

As a rule, Sampo swivels are better than imported swivels, partly because they are made from good metal. Some of the imports may look like stainless steel, but the metal will crumble under a little pressure from heavy pliers. Some imported swivels are fairly good, and seem to vary from one batch to the next, so that it's difficult to know what's what until you buy a batch and flick each one. I may be wrong, but I feel that the quality is better, on the average, from a bag of swivels (25 gross) than it is in a smaller package. Why? I hate to say it, but I believe that some manufacturers return defective swivels, or those that don't score high on the flick test. The seller might replace the swivels, but couldn't bear to throw them out, since they looked perfectly good. In other words, they are salted.

I'll also add that a swivel might work nicely when the bait is rigged, but could foul after use. The bearings grind down, especially when pulling very large blades at burbling speeds. In any case, the flick test is the only reliable guide to testing a swivel for fishing. Pick out your best ones and use them for free-falling a spinnerbait in deep water. This is the ultimate test.

Barrel Swivels. These swivels have a hollow barrel in the middle and looped wires on either end. The wire has twisted eyelets and an enlarged end, which fits inside the barrel, as shown in the drawing. Barrel swivels are inexpensive and don't score high on the flick test. They can be used, however, for making normal retrieves, but they don't work too well for rigging fall baits.

barrel swivel

Crane Swivels. These swivels have a revolving eyelet set into either end of a central housing, or barrel, as shown in the drawing. There are variations on the eyelets, but in general they aren't twisted as they are on barrel swivels. I like the design better on spinnerbaits than barrel swivels, but I admit that my preference may be based more on aesthetic considerations than on mechanical function.

crane swivel

Some time ago, R-J Tackle introduced what they called rolling swivels. These had a wider bearing surface, and were consequently much stronger than crane or barrel swivels. They worked fairly well on spinnerbaits, but aren't as good as a really good ball bearing.

Words of Wisdom. If this text tells you more than you want to know about swivels, perhaps you'll accept a few words of advice. Buy Sampo ball-bearing swivels if you're an angler or if you're making a few baits for serious anglers who know their spinnerbaits, even though the Sampo will cost more than the rest of the bait combined. Go with imported ball-bearing swivels if you're a small manufacturer trying to compete in the mass market.

At one time Sampo claimed to have the only American swivel, but Berkley has come out with what they call an American-made swivel. I haven't used these extensively on spinnerbaits, but they do look good and stand up pretty well to the flick test. Write Berkley or contact your local dealer. Also remember that things change, and that all imported swivels aren't necessarily of inferior quality.

In any case, if you're a purist who wants to eliminate the clutter on the end of a spinnerbait, I recommend a good ball-bearing swivel with split rings. But if you're a blade freak, or if you write books on fishing tackle and have to test a thousand blades, stick with snap swivels.

THE CLEVIS

A clevis is required for the front blade of a tandem-spin rigged as shown in the drawing on page 39. The exception would be to use any of the in-line blades discussed in Chapter 7, although these are seldom used on safety-pin spinnerbaits. Here are three types of clevis:

Stirrup Clevis. This design, by far the most popular for safety-pin tandem-spins, is made from a solid piece of brass with holes drilled in the ends. They're usually available only in nickel finish, but are made in several sizes. Frankly, I've never seen the larger sizes except in catalogs, and I don't see the need for them on fishing lures.

My advice is to stick with stirrup clevises for rigging safety-pin tandem-spins, especially if you're trying to market the complete spinnerbait. I normally avoid the smallest clevis on spinnerbaits, but they will work if the holes fit the wire. If you're going to have only one size of clevis, try the next one up from the smallest. In a few cases, a small clevis won't accommodate a large blade if the hole in the blade is a good distance in from the edge, as sometimes happens.

stirrup clevis

Folded Clevises. These are made from flat sheetmetal in the shape of a tiny donut, then folded, forming a semicircle with wire holes on either end. Folded clevises are frequently used on in-line spinnerbaits but not too often on tandem-spins. My objection is that the folded clevis tends to clog with silt quicker than a stirrup clevis. They're available in several sizes, which vary from one manufacturer to another, in brass, nickel, and black nickel.

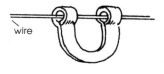

wire

folded clevis

Quick-Change Clevis. Many people want to change the front blade on a tandem-spin, but this is hard to do after the loop has been closed on the

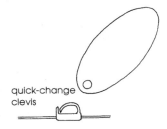

quick-change
clevis

swivel. Somebody designed a clear plastic device that permits blades to be snapped in and out, and they work pretty well, although they're too big and bulky, in my opinion. Several sizes are now available, and improvements are quite likely to come along.

BEADS AND SPACERS

Beads are used for rigging tandem spinnerbaits, and, sometimes, they're used with single-spins, although I've never figured out why. On tandem baits, the front bead keeps silt away from the clevis, and one should always be used. The bead goes between the clevis and the line-tie. I've seen spinnerbaits in components catalogs that had four beads in front of the clevis. Why?

A series of beads (or a spacer sleeve) is needed between the clevis and the swivel to put some space between the small front blade and the larger rear blade. The blades spin better if they are some distance apart. The do-it-yourselfer has a wide choice of beads and spacers, as discussed below.

hollow brass bead

Hollow Metal Beads. Several sizes of hollow brass beads are available, going from $\frac{3}{32}$ up to $\frac{1}{4}$ inch. I usually use $\frac{1}{8}$-inch beads on all spinnerbaits and $\frac{1}{8}$-ounce buzzbaits. I prefer a $\frac{1}{8}$-inch bead on all buzzbaits, but in some cases the large wire won't fit into the hole, making a $\frac{5}{32}$-inch bead necessary.

Hollow beads are usually available in nickel and polished brass. Normally I rig with nickel because most clevises are nickel plated, but suit yourself. When making your choice, don't worry about how most of the commercial baits are rigged. Manufacturers use larger beads because they are easier to string up.

Solid Metal Beads. These beads are heavy and aren't recommended for safety-pin spinnerbaits, where the extra weight up top makes the bait run on its side. They can be used in small sizes, if necessary. And beads can be very important on in-line baits because they provide casting weight and become part of the lure body.

Solid brass beads are available in a range of sizes, going by $\frac{1}{32}$ increments from $\frac{1}{8}$ to $\frac{3}{8}$ inch, in polished brass, nickel plate, and black nickel finishes. I might add that two or more of the larger solid beads can be used as a worm sinker. When the worm is twitched along, the beads click together, making a sound that many people believe attracts bass.

Plastic and Glass Beads. I've never much cared for these on safety-pin baits, but some people will use nothing else, especially the red ones. What we need, I think, is a clear plastic bead. What we've got is salmon red, lime green, dark blue, fluorescent orange, fluorescent chartreuse, and glow-in-the-dark. In shapes, we have round, oval, teardrop, and faceted. The round beads are satisfactory for blade men, but one of the oval shapes—4 x 5½ millimeters—is a great size and shape.

There are round and faceted glass beads on the market, and there is also a simulated pearl bead. These are fine for making necklaces, but for fishing tackle I prefer something that doesn't break when I overshoot the mark and cast a spinnerbait into a bridge piling.

Other Spacers. I may be wrong, but I think I was the first person to put spacer sleeves on spinnerbaits instead of beads. My firm put out thousands of these, and some small manufacturers followed suit. We used nickel-plated leader sleeves, which are widely available. Rosco makes a number of sizes, specifying the length, inside diameter, and outside diameter. Number 2 is what we normally used on tandem spinnerbaits, and it was (and is) 0.375 inch in length, 0.065 in inside diameter, and 0.086 in outside diameter. This wasn't ideal for our purpose, but it was close enough and was available as a stock item. Rosco and perhaps other manufacturers will make these to your length specification, if you're prepared to buy a large batch.

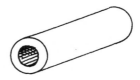

leader-sleeve spacer

Leader sleeves are normally available in plain brass, nickel plate, and black. I always use nickel. Also, some people are now using clear plastic sleeves for spacers. Try those from empty ballpoint pens.

Recommendation. I think do-it-yourselfers should stick with nickel-plated beads in ⅛-inch size if possible, and look around for some ⅛-inch beads that will fit onto 0.051-inch buzzbait wire. Manufacturers may have other ideas. I hereby admit to switching to leader sleeves when we were rigging thousands of baits and, naturally, the one-piece leader sleeve is easier to use. I'm not going to tell about the day that I knocked over a recently filled bead tray. It held 10,000 hollow, nickel-plated beads, all of which went onto the floor and rolled in all directions. Beads, beads, everywhere.

Doglegged Buzzbaits

Chapter

6

Black bass hunt their food primarily by sound instead of by sight. This fact doesn't really mean that the success of lures can always be measured in terms of noise output, and sometimes a tight wiggle will be more effective than a loose wobble. There are times, however, when a slowly retrieved noisemaker that creates a slow, rhythmic splash on the surface of the water can be deadly. Such a lure is often effective in muddy water, or at night. As a rule these lures are better when the bass (especially largemouth) are feeding in rather shallow flats instead of hiding along the bank or lazing in deep holes. On the flats, a slow, steady retrieve not only attracts the fish's attention but also helps it establish a direction, so that a hungry predator can home in from some distance away. Often a frisky bass or streaking pike will waylay a lure right at the boat, scaring the hell out of the angler.

The old Sputterfuss plug from Fred Arbogast made a lot of noise for decades, and various in-line buzzbaits—lures that chop up the surface of the water on the retrieve—were in use long ago. The leadhead buzzbaits discussed in this chapter, however, are relatively new, and most of them feature a large, high-riding, delta-shaped blade rigged on a heavy wire that is attached to a leadhead. Buzzbaits are normally dressed with rubber skirts, but bucktail, feathers, pork rind, and soft-plastic attachments are also used.

One very good thing about a buzzbait, from a manufacturer's viewpoint, is that it requires no swivel. Eliminating the swivel should permit the rigging of relatively trouble-free lures. Unfortunately, this isn't the case. An awful lot of buzzbaits simply don't work properly, even when brand new. For this reason, we'll discuss rigging and tuning at some length, along with the importance of wire design. But a buzzbait's key component is the large, noisy blade that slaps or churns the surface of the water. These come in various materials and designs, as discussed below.

Three-Wing Plastic Blades. Plastic blades have a hole running through them, from one end to the other, and the buzzbait's wire goes through the hole. As with all other buzz blades, always use a bead up front, and a pop rivet or bead in the rear. Generally, plastic blades turn freely, don't bind, and are trouble-free, if rigged properly. They are available in small, medium, and large sizes for use on ⅛-, ¼-, and ⅜- to ½-ounce baits respectively. They are also available in several colors, with or without metalflake. Anyone who doesn't want to call attention to the blade ought to consider clear plastic.

The idea behind having more than two wings on a buzz blade is the belief that a three-winged bait will "come up" faster and stay up on a slower retrieve. I have reservations about this theory, however, and I personally don't fish with metal blades with more than two wings simply because they are heavy and less than a joy to cast. In any case, there is a limit to the number of wings that will be effective on a buzzbait.

The 3-wing plastic blades work very well, and they really do keep the bait on top with a slow retrieve. I once sold some buzzbait heads to a fellow in Mechanicsville, Virginia, who rigged up some 3-wings for a handicapped angler, and he swears by them.

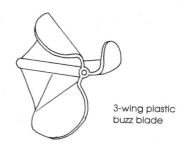

3-wing plastic
buzz blade

Four-Wing Plastic Blades. These are similar to the 3-wing blades and are available in three sizes and several colors. In my opinion, they're a bit too much of a good thing, and I really can't recommend them. They are, however, easy to rig, and then turn freely if properly rigged.

Brass Blades. These rather heavy buzz blades are available in brass or nickel finish, smooth or hammered. They're easy to rig, but they aren't available in the small, medium, and large set that bass anglers expect. Lakeland makes two sizes, and Worth makes one size. Both brands work nicely, if the wire and head are right for the blade. For whatever reason, these blades aren't very popular. The problem may be in marketing, since it's not easy for components dealers to match these to standard-size buzzbait wire and heads. The missing sizes raise too many questions to deal with.

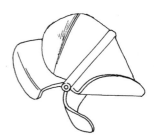

4-wing plastic buzz blade

Slotted Blades. These aluminum blades, similar in overall shape to the brass blades, have front and back tabs, one up and one down, and a long slot through the blade so that the buzzbait wire goes through one tab, through the slot, and out the other tab. These blades are available in two sizes for ¼- and ⅜-ounce heads; they're not very common and aren't my personal favorites.

Counter-turning Blades. These aluminum blades are designed to be used in tandem: one turns clockwise while the other turns counterclockwise. They are available in two sizes, one for ¼-ounce baits and one for ⅜- and ½-ounce baits. They can be rigged on standard wire, usually with a bead up front, a bead in the middle, and a pop rivet on the end, as discussed later. Although the blades work nicely, they aren't my favorite because they make more of

counter buzz blade

a chop in the water rather than the steady plop-plop-plop that I want. They do, however, run quite straight if rigged correctly. These and other double-bladed buzzbaits are covered later in this chapter.

Lunker Lure Blades. I don't know what to call these blades, but the first ones that I saw were on the old Lunker Lure, one of the first doglegged buzzbaits to gain national importance. It's a very good blade, and it has caught many fish. Essentially, it is a delta-shaped aluminum blade, with bent-down tabs on either end. The tabs are drilled, so that the buzzbait wire goes through the center of the tabs. Since the tabs are bent the same way, the blade is slightly offset. It works, though, and produces a nice plop-plop-plop on a steady retrieve. Blades of this design are available in three sizes from some of the component suppliers.

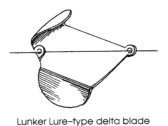

Lunker Lure–type delta blade

Quad Blades. These four-bladed buzzbaits are made by putting two sections together—two tabbed blades of the lunker lure design with wings bent to 90 degrees instead of 180. The luremaker puts two blades together and strings them up onto the buzzbait wire. Quad blades are available in ⅛-, ¼-, and ⅜- to ½-ounce sizes. The blades work, but they are too heavy, hard to store, and they don't have the plop-plop-plop of regular 2-wing delta blades.

Classic Blades. These blades have become pretty much standard in the industry and are my personal favorites. They're similar to the Lunker Lure blades, except that the front tab is bent one way and the rear tab is bent

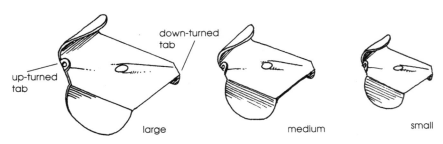

Standard Aluminum Buzz Blades

the other. The buzzbait wire runs through a hole in the center of the blade and a channel formed on either end, running from the tab to the center hole. If you've got the right blade, the right wire, and the right components, these blades are ideal. I don't know who designed these blades, but the first ones I ever saw came from James Sparkmen in Missouri.

Available in three sizes to fit the popular ⅛-, ¼-, and ⅜- or ½-ounce heads and standard wire, they usually come in aluminum finish, but painted or anodized finishes are sometimes available. These finishes seem to come and go for one reason or another, but the plain aluminum finish is clearly the standard finish in the buzzbait business and suits me fine.

Fast Buzz Blades. One of my favorite lures for fishing fast is the Harrison-Hoge Weedwing. Essentially, it's a spoon with small, swept-back blades up front, and it has to be retrieved fast to keep it on top. It can be deadly on bass, however, in spite of the generally good advice to slow down. As far as I know, no such blades are available as components, but the do-it-yourselfer might experiment with the larger propeller blades bent back to make a 20-degree angle with the axis of rotation.

RIGGING BUZZBAITS

Usually, buzzbaits are assembled with a pop rivet on the rear and a bead up front, as shown in the drawing. Although some luremakers omit it, the front bead helps keep moss and algae and water scum from clogging up the blade. The pop rivet on the rear keeps the blade away from the down-turned wire end. The rivet itself can be rigged loose, free to move up and down the wire a bit, or it can be fixed by crimping it onto the wire. Crimping prevents the pop rivet from turning. When the pop rivet can't turn, it causes friction on the blade's rear tab; some say this produces a squealing sound on the retrieve, and buzzbaits rigged in this manner are sometimes called squealers. The squealer might have come about by accident, however, instead of by design. A bead used on the rear of the wire tends to slip around the wire and come off. A pop rivet won't slip off, and it was probably first used merely to hold on the blade. (A leader sleeve would have done the same thing.) I might add that a bead *can* be used if the right bend is put into the wire, and I once had a steady customer who simply would not fish with any bait with a pop rivet on it. Maybe he figured all that squealing scared the bass away. Sometimes, however, a burr on the head will keep the blade from turning properly.

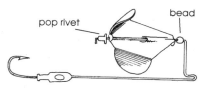

    Buzz blades that are not carefully rigged may not turn freely. Turning a tight blade by hand, or by blowing on it, sometimes helps it start rotating. In effect, repeated turning wears away a little of the aluminum on the blade, so that, up to a point, the more the blade turns the smoother it goes. Someone hit on the idea of holding a buzzbait out a car window, letting the wind do the work. On a TV show out in Texas, John Fox picked up on this and popularized the notion that a buzzbait had to be broken in. I don't remember the exact formula, but it was somewhere in the neighborhood of traveling 15 miles distance at 55 miles per hour. I know one fellow who used an air hose to "break in" the blade. But if everything turns freely to start with, no breaking-in period is necessary, I say.

    When rigging the bait, be certain that the blade, bead, and rivet aren't too tight. Bending the end of the wire down to hold the pop rivet can easily bind the blade so that it doesn't turn freely. This happens quite often, possibly because the wire is heavy and hard to bend with ordinary pliers, especially when you have only a very short wire end sticking out of the pop rivet.

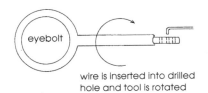

wire is inserted into drilled
hole and tool is rotated

If you have a problem, using longer wire will help, but, on the other hand, you don't want any more wire sticking down than necessary. Also, using a smaller bead up front will sometimes solve the problem. Usually, ⁵⁄₃₂-inch beads are used. Going to ⅛ inch will gain ¹⁄₃₂ inch, but some brands of ⅛-inch beads won't fit onto the large-diameter buzzbait wire. A bending tool adequate for the job will help, and my nephew, David Livingston, designed a simple device from an eyebolt that will bend 0.051-inch wire. It's easy to make one. First, file or grind flattened surfaces on the end of the bolt. Drill a hole (or several holes) through the bolt, as shown in the drawing. Ideally, the hole should be just a tad larger than the diameter of the wire.

Still another problem occurs when the holes drilled into the buzz blades aren't properly aligned during manufacture. Unless you make your own blades, you won't have control of this, and will have to rig the blades you can get. Sometimes bending the front and rear tabs a bit, usually with the end of the buzzbait wire, will help. The holes can be drilled out, but this takes a lot of time. The root of the problem isn't the diameter of the tab holes, however; it's the alignment. Merely bending the blade by putting pressure in the middle will sometimes help, if you bend from the correct side and don't overdo it.

In any case, the blade must turn freely if the buzzbait is to do its thing, and all buzzbaits should be tested immediately after rigging. The usual test is to gently blow on the blade or flick it gently with the finger. In either case, the key word is *gently*. Some blades seem to work fine at high speed, but bind up when slowed down to fishing speeds.

Usually, the "binding" problem is more common with blades that have reversed tabs at either end.

BUZZBAIT WIRE

An important consideration, too often overlooked, is whether or not the lure will hook fish effectively. Some buzzbaits won't, and no doubt this helped promote the notion of using trailer or "stinger" hooks. Ideally, a buzzbait should have plenty of "bite," or gap, between blade and hook point without your having to resort to a trailer hook.

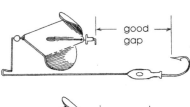

good gap

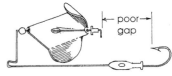

poor gap

Personally, I simply don't use lures that have the blade too close to the hook's point. Period. On the other hand, I must point out that tackle shops across the land have stocked millions of well-known brand-name buzzbaits with scant gap, and they must catch fish somehow in order to keep selling. One well-known lure company even put a buzz blade onto a short-armed spinnerbait, making it almost impossible for a bass or other gamefish to get at the hook. These baits were packaged and put on the market without a trailer hook attached, and no doubt many people fished them. Not me. But not for a minute do I doubt whether bass will hit them!

More often than not, very heavy wire, 0.051 inch in diameter, is used on buzzbaits. To form an eyelet, wire of this gauge must be bent into some form of open eye, usually an R. Such heavy wire precludes the use of a twisted eye, and for that reason a few people have switched to lighter buzzbait wire, usually 0.040 inch in diameter. One big advantage of the lighter wire is that it bends easier, the blades turn on it better, and binding isn't as much of a problem. A big disadvantage is that the light wire is easy to bend and hard to keep tuned.

THE BALANCING ACT

Buzzbaits worthy of the name must churn water on the retrieve. Usually, the bigger the blade, the more noise it makes. But if the blade is too large for the weight of the head, the bait will run to the left or right on the retrieve. It is therefore desirable to have a *heavy* head.

But a heavy head makes the bait slow to "come up," and a faster retrieve is needed to keep it on top. It is therefore desirable, in this regard, to have a *light* head. Obviously, good buzzbait design is a compromise, and most thinking people settle for a bait that comes up fast and stays on top on a slow retrieve, but may run off to the side a bit on a faster retrieve.

Generally, buzzbaits are sized as small, medium, and large. A small blade is sized for a ⅛-ounce head and wire bent especially for this blade; a medium blade for a ¼-ounce head and wire; and a large blade for a ⅜- to ½-ounce head and wire. The wire is part of the plan because the larger blades won't fit on the smaller wires.

There is a considerable difference in the actual weight of the heads from the various manufacturers. One problem is that manufacturers want their bait to run perfectly straight and tend to increase the weight of the head. Personally, I don't object to a lure running a little to the right or left, and some people want them to do just that. Or say they do. It is, I allow, sometimes possible to fish a wandering lure "into" a line of brush or perhaps a rock wall. Trouble is, you might need a lure that veers to the right on one cast, and one that goes left on the next.

One trick that will help buzzbaits stay on track is bending up the top wire slightly. This drops the leadhead down, thereby better balancing the torque created by the top-riding blade. I fish such a lure frequently, and I like it because it puts the head and skirt down under the water a bit, making it more visible to fish. Since the skirt covers the hook, that's the part of the buzzbait that I want the fish to see.

DOUBLE BUZZERS

As stated earlier, some buzz blades are designed to be used in tandem on the same shaft. One turns clockwise and the other turns counterclockwise. When first introduced, these created a flurry, but the blades never did become as popular as one might have thought. They chop the water up quite a bit, but the essential "plop, plop, plop" is missing.

When I had a tackle shop, a luremaker and tackle tinkerer from Ohio once showed me a buzzbait he'd made by soldering a two-legged wire to a

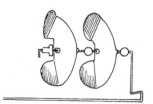

rigged counter blades

double buzz

regular buzzbait. It had two delta-shaped blades, one that rotated one way and one that went the other. He didn't much like it when I didn't agree with his thinking on the matter. A year or so later he came back, this time with a new wrinkle. He had put two blades on each leg of the wire! That's four blades on one buzzbait. My reaction was close enough to a laugh to upset the guy.

"They'll catch bass!" he shouted at me over the cash register.

Well, I never doubted that. But I can't imagine trying to cast the thing all day. Two-bladed buzzbaits tend to gain altitude, like a twin-engine airplane, and go their own way. You need a remote control to guide the cast.

I saw my first twin-bladed buzzbait hanging on a pegboard in a Kmart store. It had small, bright styrene floats inserted over the wire between blade and rivet. Years later I talked with a good ol' boy who was about to put a version of these float baits on the market, and he wanted me to distribute some for him.

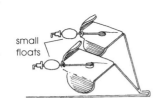
small floats

"These baits," he explained, "come up fast and stay up on a slow retrieve."

Of course I'd heard the pitch many times before, and as one bullshitter to another, I asked how slow.

"Well," he said, "I've actually seen 'em run backwards!"

In any case, the twin buzzbait design, with a blade side by side, is difficult to manufacture, difficult to package, difficult to keep in a tackle box, and difficult to cast accurately. One advantage of the design is that, if counter-turning blades are used, the lures do indeed run straight.

HEAD KNOCKERS AND TICKERS

Sound and splash or surface chop, not color, is what made buzzbaits popular in the first place. They're quite effective on dark nights partly because they attract bass and other gamefish and partly because the sound of the large blade churning the water helps anglers communicate with the lure. When anglers hear the "plop, plop, plop" they know that their bait is working properly, and have a bearing on its whereabouts. For these reasons, the large delta blades are hard to beat for night fishing.

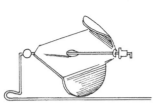
blade makes ticking sound

But ever since the pop rivet was pooped up as producing a squealing noise against the turn of the blade, the buzzbait has been the tackle tinkerer's dream. By design or by accident, the blade can be bent down a bit so that it hits on the wire; now we've got a lure that goes "plop, plop, plop," "squeak, squeak, squeak," and "tick, tick, tick."

head knocker with trailer hook

At some point, somebody dropped the blade back so that it would knock against the head of the lure, and there are several variations on the head-knocker design. Some use a short wire, as shown in the drawing; others use a long wire with a long blade arm. Either wire design puts the blade over the head—and close to the hook. Too close to suit me. Apart from questionable hook bite, most head knockers and wire tickers don't work if the wire is bent up or down a fraction of an inch. In short, they require frequent hand tuning while fishing.

Another design makes use of some sort of large bead or sound chamber fixed onto the buzzbait wire. The first one of these I saw came from a fellow by the name of Billy Johnson, a good ol' boy from Americus, Georgia, who knew Billy Carter. It was made from an ordinary buzzbait, but Billy had installed a loose sleeve, adapted from a metal tube salvaged from a ballpoint pen, that was cut to proper length and fitted onto the wire between the blade and the head. The last such rattle chamber I saw was a large bead that had rattle pellets in it. When shaken, the thing sounded like a maraca.

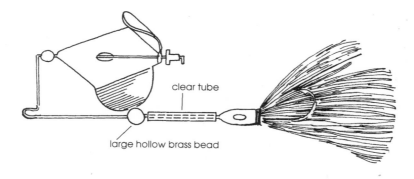

clear tube

large hollow brass bead

Some rattle chambers are fixed to the wire immediately behind the blade, and others (not shown) are free-floating between blade and line tie. My favorite design has a clear plastic tube (taken from an empty ballpoint pen) between the bead and the head.

Another kind of noisemaker makes use of an attachment dropped back from the front of the bait. Spinner blades are frequently used, especially willowleafs; they're attached to the front wire and are free to flop about. On the retrieve the spinner blade rises up and clanks against the buzz blade. There are various ways to rig such a bait, but usually beads or spacers are used on either side of the blade. Ideally, such a clanker should be partly

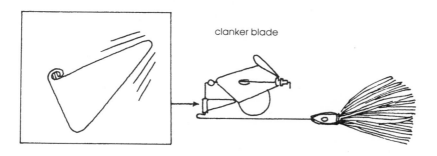

clanker blade

rigged before the wire is bent. This causes something of a problem for those of us who work with preformed wire. Many small manufacturers and hobbyists straighten out preformed wire, rig it with a clanker blade, and rebend it.

After the use of a spinner blade on a buzzbait was accepted, somebody came up with a special clanker blade, designed for use on a buzzbait. These are now manufactured in large numbers, and other designs are certain to follow, in several colors.

Another ticker bait I've seen was sent to me from Pennsylvania. It is relatively easy to rig, once you get the hang of it. This design makes use of a rather long blade-arm wire, and the blade, a standard 3-wing plastic design, is free to move up and down the wire a bit. (Rigging it too tightly will kill the action.) The end of the buzzbait wire is bent around and back toward the blade. On the retrieve, the 3-wing blade slides back as it starts turning, and the blade's wings hit the end of the wire. This contact makes a "tick" sound, and kicks the blade forward slightly. The blade slides back, and another tick comes when the next wing hits the wire. A steady retrieve produces a "tick, tick, tick," if all goes according to plan.

HOOKS AND HEADS

As a rule, buzzbait hooks are similar to spinnerbait hooks, and are more or less interchangeable. A good many people rig trailer hooks onto buzzbaits, and, indeed, they are required with some short-wire baits where the blade is very close to the head. It's best in my opinion to move the blade forward so that bass and other gamefish can get hold of the main hook.

Usually, a buzzbait head isn't bullet shaped like a spinnerbait's, but is more or less flattened, the general belief being that a flat-headed bait will stay up better on a slow retrieve. While there may be some truth to this, the difference is so small as to be academic, except that whatever anglers really believe determines how much confidence they have in their lure. In the past, several baits have been made with flat heads, but they're usually made from brass or some hard alloy. Leadheads can be flattened with the aid of a hammer or an arbor press, as discussed in Chapter 3.

OTHER BUZZBAITS

Another kind of buzzbait features an in-line blade and often has a weed-guard of one sort or another. These baits are discussed in more detail in Chapter 7, along with the wire attachments that can be used on such in-line lures. Because this chapter deals with top-riding blades and doglegged wire forms, I include the next lure here. Perhaps I risk outlandishness by including it at all, but the fact is that many bass anglers have hitched sonic vibrator-type lures, such as the Rattletrap, onto a top-riding buzz-blade harness. This was something of a craze in parts of North Carolina a while back, and the fellows who didn't have them were melting the lead off regular

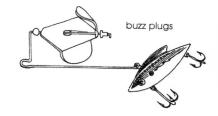

buzz plugs

buzzbaits. If you rig some from new wire or rob some old buzzbaits, make sure that the gap at the wire-loop connection is closed down tight. Some twisting fish, such as the devious and devilish bowfin, can undo the lure from the wire.

I don't care to fish with anything like Rattletraps harnessed to buzz blades, and of course the long-term popularity of the design remains to be proved. Meanwhile, many such rigs will be thrown into American waters—and anything that doesn't like them will quite likely get a mouthful of hooks.

In-Line Spinnerbaits and Buzzbaits

O
ne advantage of a safety-pin spinnerbait is that the leadhead drops down much lower than the line-tie eyelet. This keel-like design makes the lure less likely to twist the line on the retrieve. Indeed, line twist is a common problem with many in-line baits—a problem that causes bird's nests and other casting problems, especially with monofilament line on a spinning reel. Also, remember that doglegged spinners work better as fall baits, for reasons already discussed at some length.

On the other hand, in-line baits of proper design are better for working very close to a shoreline or casting to visible cover, and they certainly go into and out of brush with fewer hangups. Remember that on the cast the safety-pin bait goes in backward, with the V shape of the wire wide open like a mouth. If the top arm touches a twig, the hook end flips up and hangs. Some in-lines with rabbit-ear weedguards do the same thing, but some of these are designed to flop over somewhat. Other weedguard designs are better for casting to visible cover, and at the end of this chapter I set forth a design that I consider to be ideal.

Some in-line spinnerbaits have lead molded around a wire shaft. Others are made with brass or lead weights of various shapes with a hole in the middle; these are merely strung up onto a wire shaft. Still others are made by molding lead onto a hook, then attaching the hook eyelet to a detachable spinner-blade arm. Each of the three types has advantages and disadvantages.

Hawaiian Wiggler with flip-up weedguard

Slip-on Bodies. A good many in-line spinnerbaits, such as the popular Mepps lures, aren't made with normal lead molds but are instead put together with brass weights and other such pieces. Sometimes more than one piece is used, and, in fact, one components catalog lists dozens of weights and shapes. The solid brass beads, available from ⅛ inch in diameter all the way up to ½ inch in diameter, are satisfactory for some in-lines.

Although the Mepps-type lures are made in sizes big enough to interest

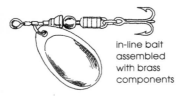

in-line bait assembled with brass components

in-line lure bodies

largemouth bass, and in giant sizes for muskies, most of these baits are used for trout and panfish. Others, such as the Rooster Tail and the Shyster, are also used, more often than not, for crappie or white bass. Lures of this type used for largemouth and other black bass are more likely to have a weedguard of some sort. Usually, this is a rabbit-ear or V-shaped antenna-type weedguard, such as the one on the Snagless Sally–type lures. These work pretty well, but they do require lots of adjusting during a fishing trip, especially in waters where bowfin are plentiful.

Another problem with the V guard is that it tends to make the bait ride upside down from the way I want it to ride. The weight of the guard makes the lure hook point ride down or to the side instead of up. This puts the weedguard sticking down where it can get in the way when the fish tries to take the bait. I much prefer to have a weedguard that fits in closer to the hook, as on the weedless Johnson's Silver Minnow spoon. It is, it seems to me, more trouble-free.

Weighted-Hook In-Lines. I prefer in-line lures of this type because the weight is cast around the hook and because weedguards can be built in instead of using the rabbit-ear flop-up design. Such lures, having a low profile, cast into brush better than any others. They're hard to find on the market, but do-it-yourselfers can come up with their own designs. I might add that some weighted-hook in-lines do have rabbit-ear weedguards. The famous old Hawaiian Wiggler comes readily to mind. These are good lures, but I really prefer a different weedguard concept.

Sometimes, you can make good in-line spinners by combining other lures with a spinner-arm attachment (discussed later in this chapter). Some weedless spoons, for example, make very good in-line baits if the right attachment is used.

Some jig molds can be modified easily to make in-line heads. To visualize this, merely look at a certain jig (or at the mold) and imagine how it would work if a wire ran out the nose instead of out the top of the head. You can cut a wire channel into the mold and connect it to a spinnerbait hook. See Chapter 9 for how-to tips on modifying molds.

Remember that not all jig molds work as nicely as others for making an in-line. A banana-jig head, for example, makes a very good in-line design because it has a heavy belly, which makes the bait run straight without twisting. One important point to consider is whether or not the lure will be a good hooker. To this end, I would discourage anyone from making a lure of this type from a jig, and especially one in which the hook has a 90-degree bend. Such a lure will surely draw strikes, but the hooking percentage won't be as good as with a similar lure with a better bite.

Anyone who has the notion of using a spinnerbait or buzzbait mold with a straight wire in it, or who modifies a jig mold to accommodate a hook and straight-wire shaft, should consider the matter carefully. The resulting lure may look good in the water and may indeed attract fish; I have known anglers who wanted such straight-wire baits and could not be talked out of the notion. But I really can't go along with the practice because it's difficult for a fish to get a straight-wire rig in its mouth. Think about it. If the lure measures 4 inches from line tie to hook point, then the fish's mouth would have to be 4 inches wide to take in the whole works if it hit broadside. (Some stick plugs are that long, but remember that they have treble hooks sticking out every which way.) Of course, a bass or other fish could get at the hook from the rear, but I feel that a fish shouldn't have to work at getting hooked. Clearly, a jointed bait will work better in this regard, especially for working in heavy cover.

In any case, if you use a long-shanked hook in such a mold, it is better to use one with bait-holder barbs on the shank, so that the head won't twist around. Some worm hooks will also work, along with Tru-Turns and S-shaped hooks designed for use on cork-bodied bugs. Also remember that part of the eye of the hook can be inside the lead, which will also prevent the head from turning on the shank; a large hook eye works better for this purpose.

Weight-Forward In-Line Baits. The modern Eerie Dearie lures, often used for walleye, are good examples of baits of this type. Basically they consist of a straight-wire shaft with a casting weight on one end and a dressed hook on the other, with a spinner of some sort rigged in between. Inexpensive molds as well as preformed wires are readily available for these lures.

I won't go into great detail here on rigging, but notice that the blade is spaced well above the hook so that it can turn freely. This spacing can be accomplished with beads or with a spacer of some sort, or with a built-in snap-on system. The hook can be dressed with Living Rubber, hair, feathers, or what have you. Some of these lures, however, are fished with a bare hook, without dressing, in which case the spinner blade is the main attractor. Some of these lures have painted heads, complete with eyes, to add to the attraction. Often, the head and the hook aren't widely separated, so that the fish can get the whole thing into its mouth.

The first lure of this type that I ever fished extensively was the old Paul Bunyan, which was jointed in some way. My older brother

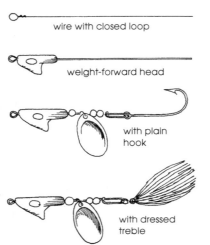

wire with closed loop

weight-forward head

with plain hook

with dressed treble

told me not to throw the thing into the old Hicks Dead River, lest a big ol' grinnel bite it in half. What I hooked was surely a grinnel. I don't know quite what the fish did, but I reeled in only half the Paul Bunyan.

The second lure of this type that I ever fished was The Thing, a light lure made by the Columbia Company. It was a snap-on lure, and the company rigged it with a #8 foam-rubber spider with legs. Since bluegills feed primarily on insects (and most such spinner lures end up looking more like minnows), The Thing was a truly great lure for these tasty fish, as well as similar panfish. I highly recommend this design, rigged on a 3/16-ounce head, a size 0 or size 1 blade, and a size 10 spider. The spiders can be purchased from tackle shops or firms that market fly-fishing lures. I prefer black spiders with white legs, but several colors are available. Do-it-yourselfers can purchase sponge rubber bodies in several colors, and make the rubber legs from Living Rubber skirt material. Any spinnerbaitmaker will have lots of scraps that are suitable for spiders. Fly tyers can come up with a thousand wet-fly designs for fishing on such a rig.

The Thing

The possibilities for weight-forward lures are almost limitless. One main advantage is that these lures don't often twist the line, even while trolling, because of the offset, bottom-heavy, keel-shaped leadhead. The blade works fairly well with this arrangement, provided that it doesn't hang up on the lure's dressing or hook. In other words, the blade should be spaced properly.

The big disadvantage of the weight-forward design is that such lures are easy for some head-shaking fish to throw. On Lake Weir in Florida I once tied into three bass on three successive casts, only to have them jump up, shake their heads, and sling the lure back at me. Fish that don't jump, like bluegills, aren't as likely to throw the lures.

As a rule, these baits are fished in relatively deep water. If the bait is allowed to free-fall, nose down, the spinner blade (if things are balanced) will turn and slow it down, which may be the reason for the blade's great success. (The spinner blade on a regular in-line bait doesn't normally turn on the fall.) As a fall bait, however, it isn't as good as the single-spin or safety-pin design.

This lure is often fished very slowly along the bottom, and I suspect that, as often as not, the spinner blade isn't even working half the time. (If it is, I can't feel it.) In this case, the blade may act more as a visual attractor than as a source of vibration. Perhaps this explains why it's not popular as a largemouth lure.

BLADES FOR IN-LINES

One problem with in-line baits is that the blade doesn't turn as readily as a blade on the end of a doglegged spinnerbait. Remember that the blade isn't attached to a swivel, and must swing completely around the wire. (The front blade on a top-riding tandem-spin must also turn around on its shaft, but in this case the angle of the shaft is different and the blade is usually much smaller.) As a rule, the larger the blade the harder it is to start turning; sometimes, a little twitch of the rod tip at the beginning of the retrieve is necessary to get it going.

All manner of standard spinner blades are used on in-line baits, including Colorado, Indiana, willowleaf, and others, such as ripple blades and swing blades. In addition, some special blades are made for use exclusively on in-line baits. Most of these stand out from the shaft and turn at a fixed angle, as discussed below.

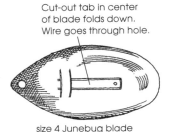

Cut-out tab in center of blade folds down. Wire goes through hole.

size 4 Junebug blade

Junebug. These old blades are not often used today, but they should be, and are still available in several sizes. As shown in the drawing, a strip of the middle of the blade is cut out and folded down, and a hole is drilled in the end for the wire. The folded-down strip forms a stand-off that keeps the blade sticking out at a fixed angle. The angle can be varied somewhat, depending on how far down the strip is bent. (Lakeland ships them with the leg unbent, and I have even seen these on safety-pin spinnerbaits.) The greater the bend, the more resistance the blade has; the more resistance, the higher the bait rides, other things being equal. Thus, if you want to fish deep on a certain retrieve, close in the angle. If you want to fish shallow with the same retrieve, open out the blade. But be careful not to bind the blade with an extreme angle either way.

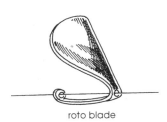

roto blade

Roto Blades. These blades use a fixed hollow shaft as a bearing, and the whole works revolves around the spinnerbait wire. They have a fixed angle, but can be bent a little to adjust the action.

Do-it-yourselfers should know that it's possible to rig standard blades roto-style on a leader sleeve. It's best to have a leader sleeve that fits rather snugly into the hole in the blade, and one that has a small inside diameter. The trick is to insert the leader sleeve about halfway through the hole and solder it in place. This can usually be done without special tools, but it's hard to get the exact angle every time unless you rig some sort of jig for holding blade and sleeve in place. If you aren't rigged for soldering, try epoxy putty. Superglue might even work for a cast or two, at least for experimenting with angles and so on. Try a water-resistant gap-filling glue such as Zap-a-Gap.

in-line blade

In-Line Blades. I don't know what exactly to call these blades, but Lakeland markets them under the name "in-line." The first ones I ever saw were on the Panther Martin baits. In any case, the idea is to have a small hole, set at a certain angle, drilled in such a spot that both the top and the bottom parts of the blade contribute to the rotation.

Propeller Blades. Available in several sizes, these are sometimes rigged on a shaft ahead of a fly or dressed treble hook. They can also be used in front of weighted casting spinners, and are especially useful on the 1/16- to 1/8-ounce lures designed for crappie, where the blade needs to turn on a slow retrieve. Crappie lures should be dressed with white feathers or bucktail, usually

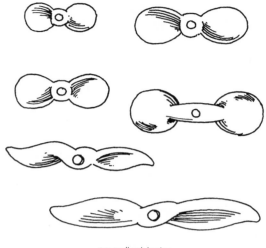

propeller blades

about 1½ inches long. Propeller blades can be rigged close to the lure, but they hook better if they are a ways ahead of the hook. They are often rigged in tandem.

WIRE FOR IN-LINE SPINNERS

There are various schemes for rigging in-line baits, and various manufacturers have their own ways of doing things, some of which may be difficult for the do-it-yourselfer to duplicate without the aid of special wire-working equipment. Consequently, I feel that hobbyists ought to think in terms of detachable spinner arms. These can be made from straight wire, and one can purchase partly formed wire shafts with one end already formed. The standard pieces are shown at right.

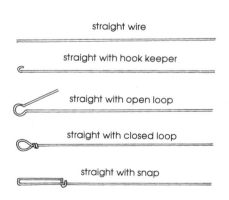

straight wire

straight with hook keeper

straight with open loop

straight with closed loop

straight with snap

Of course, straight wire can be used and is more versatile, especially if you have a wire-bending tool or jig. In any case, there are three basic designs for detachable spinner arms. All have a loop formed for the line tie; they vary in how the wire attaches to the hook or head (of course, the rigging also varies). I have classified these according to this connection.

Twisted-Loop Eyelets. The strongest and most foolproof of all the connections, this is essentially a piece of wire, rigged with clevis, blades, and beads, with a loop on either end. The wire is attached to the hook or lure eyelet directly or with the aid of a split ring. Once attached, there is little danger that a grinnel or some such tackle buster will unhook it. The problem is that split-ring construction makes it a little difficult to change the

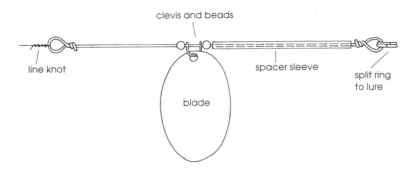

hook or head; it's usually easier to change lures. Spinner-arm attachments of this type aren't often available in tackle shops, simply because they are not snap-ons and require an intermediate split ring. Serious tackle tinkerers, however, can make their own and will know how to use split rings.

Snap-On. These are the kind of spinners usually marketed in tackle shops, especially by Hildrebrandt and Lindy's. They are satisfactory and easy to use on weighted flies and similar heads. My problem is that I never trust them, and end up squeezing the wire shut with pliers. Notice that these wires are available already formed on the snap end, so that one need only string up bead, clevis, blade, and another bead. The snap part also acts as a stand-off to keep the blade ahead of the lure head. When attaching such a bait, remember to keep the bead ahead of the snap part so that it will keep the clevis turning freely.

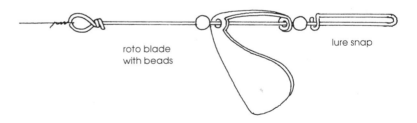

It's fairly easy to bend snap-on wire shafts from scratch, which will give you more control over the length of the snap arm. Most of the commercial models are made with rather light wire. If you bend your own, try one made with 0.035-inch stainless steel wire.

Coil-Spring Lock. This connection is sometimes used in the fishing-tackle trade. It's a strong connection—if everything works right—but I don't recommend it. Invariably, rust is a problem, and I have fished with some springs that tended to come off. Note carefully that the spring must be the right size for the wire in order to have a snug fit, and that the wire should

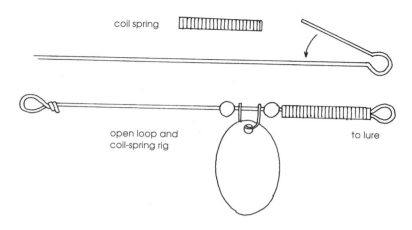

have a good deal of tension on it. Usually, this tension is provided by the angle of the bend. Further, a good deal depends on the diameter and spring-back strength of the wire. I recommend that the wire be at least 0.030-inch stainless steel.

These spinner arms are easy to rig, once you have the right bend in the wire. If the blade is to turn freely, it's always best to have at least one bead between the spring and the clevis. A stand-off sleeve or additional beads may be required to space the blade at a suitable distance away from the head and skirt.

IN-LINE BUZZBAITS

Doglegged buzzbaits with top-riding blades (discussed in Chapter 6) are very popular these days for fishing in shallow or muddy water, day and night. Another class of buzzbaits, usually called in-lines, is much older. In-lines have the blade attached in front of the weighted head and are dressed with Living Rubber, bucktail, and so on. I like these baits very much—if they are jointed and if the blade is sufficiently far from the head. Both of the "ifs" have to do with the bait's ability to hook fish. Obviously, a large delta blade whirling directly in front of the hook can cause missed strikes.

Actually, any of the rigs discussed under in-line spinnerbaits can be adapted for buzzbaits simply by using a suitable blade, or blades, in the case of a tandem buzz. Many of the commercial baits of this type have rabbit-ear weedguards, and the do-it-yourselfer can easily modify molds to make a suitable bait with fiber- or Y-shaped weedguards.

Since the baits should be jointed, and since the blade should ride a good ways ahead of the head, I think it's best for the do-it-yourselfer to think in terms of buzzbait attachments. The connection part is identical to those on spinner attachments, and the sketches on page 64 show how the blades should be rigged.

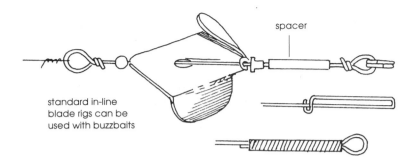

spacer

standard in-line
blade rigs can be
used with buzzbaits

Buzz blades are made in several sizes, usually small (suitable for ⅛-ounce baits), medium (¼-ounce), large (⅜-ounce), and extra large (½-ounce). It's possible to switch sizes and lure weights, but of course a small blade attached to a ½-ounce leadhead will have to be retrieved fast to keep it on top. Conversely, a large blade on a light head will have too much torque and the lure will run off to the side instead of coming straight in.

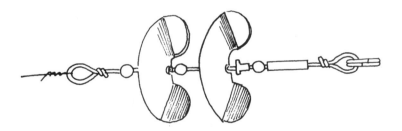

Tandem buzz blades can also be rigged on in-line baits, and they work nicely if a set of clockwise and counterclockwise blades are used. These should be rigged with a stand-off, spacer, and front bead. The middle spacer can also be a bead or two.

Regardless of your personal choice of blades and how you prefer to rig them, remember that buzz attachments can be fished with a variety of lures, or even with hooks rigged with stick-on pork frogs and soft-plastic attachments. Spoons can be deadly when fished behind a buzz attachment, and in-line lure bodies can also be used. Even plugs can be fished behind buzz attachments. Stick plugs without diving lips are very easy to rig and fish. And don't count out the plugs with diving lips; these can be rigged by removing the rear hook and attaching it to the line-tie eyelet. The lip actually gives the plug a slight side-to-side motion behind the buzz blade; this rig can be deadly on largemouth bass.

One of my favorite in-line buzz rigs is a small buzz blade rigged ahead of a pork fork. The frog tends to make the lure ride high on a slow retrieve,

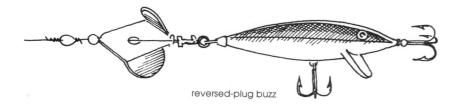

reversed-plug buzz

and, having a pork belly, provides weight for casting. It's best to trim the front of the frog a little, making it plane better. I also tie a little deer hair or other dressing onto the hook, mostly for the benefit of lure presentation. A little hair provides air resistance, which slows the lure down on the cast and makes for a gentler splashdown. It's deadly. Try it. And hold on.

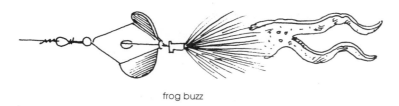

frog buzz

The pork frog and dressed hook can also be used behind a spinner-blade attachment.

THE BAMA BUG STORY

Back when I was in the fishing-lure business, I designed and put into production what I considered to be the world's best in-line bait. It could readily be adapted to a number of spinner-arm configurations, including buzzers. I called it the Bama Bug, but ran into problems with the name because the head was so versatile. It was a system, really, and I still say it's the best ever.

We manufactured several thousand of the baits, but for various reasons I got out of the lure business before the idea caught on. And it might never have caught on in a big way. Because a bait catches fish and works well doesn't mean that it will be a commercial success. One of the best baits I ever designed, the Bass Nymph-O, simply didn't sell. You couldn't give the damned things away. In any case, the Bama Bug, as I dubbed it, did work very well—and still does. The basic head is shown at right.

Notice that most of the weight of the head is below the projected centerline of hook and wire. In other words, it has more weight on the bottom than on top, which makes it ride with the

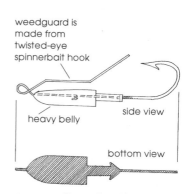

weedguard is made from twisted-eye spinnerbait hook

side view

heavy belly

bottom view

Bama Bug Head

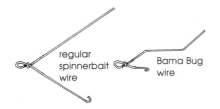

regular
spinnerbait
wire

Bama Bug
wire

hook point up. This keeps it from twisting the line and makes it almost weedless without any sort of weedguard. What weedguard there is also keeps the pork-rind trailer from flopping around and sticking onto the point.

The weedguard is actually made from a safety-pin spinnerbait wire that has a very short bottom leg and a doglegged top, as shown at left.

This wire is hooked up and molded just like a regular spinnerbait. When it comes out of the mold, the wire sticks out oddly, where it stays until after all the painting and dressing. Then the wire is bent over until it almost touches the point of the hook.

This bait can be rigged with double blades as well as single blades, and one of my favorite combinations is a small and large presto blade.

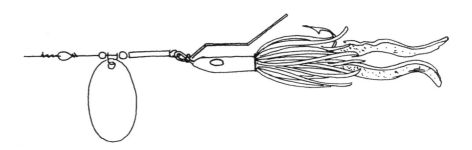

The flat shape of the Bama Bug permits the head to be a little wider than a round head of the same weight, giving the hook point more side protection, which I felt was needed because of the single weedguard wire. Also, the flat head prevents the lure from rolling over on the hook when it's pulled across limbs, which can be quite important in a shallow-water in-line bait. Thus, the flat head contributes to the bait's weedlessness, and permits the weedguard to go all the way down even with the dogleg. This shape of weedguard makes it much easier to set the hook, while at the same time providing enough protection for the hook's point.

The flat head also makes the Bama Bug work very, very nicely as a buzzbait, the flat head causing the bait to ride higher on a slower retrieve. When I marketed the lure, it was more popular as a buzzbait than as a spinnerbait, but I never quite knew why. I normally rigged it with a ¼-ounce blade, and it worked very well and stayed up on a slow retrieve. It also worked nicely with a medium-size 3-wing plastic blade, although I prefer aluminum blades for fishing.

Finally, I like to fish the Bama Bug as a fall bait, dressed with bucktail or fitted with a shad-shaped, soft-plastic attachment. The key, of course, is to use a jig spinner with a size 3½ or 4 Colorado blade. This makes a nice rig for fishing deep for suspended bass. The flat head behaves rather differently from an ordinary leadhead jig, as slider-jig fans know, and I like this

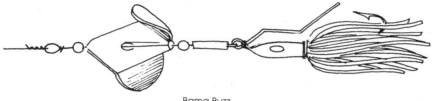

Bama Buzz

rig as a fall bait in medium-depth water (15 feet or so). When used in this manner, it will stick more fish if the weedguard is snipped off.

The head of the Bama Bug also makes the best rig I've ever used for fishing plastic worms. I have never liked to fish with the Texas rig and have blasted it for 30 years, whenever I could find an editor willing to buck the trend. The Texas rig is weedless, all right, but it's also difficult to stick a fish with it. For many years every bass pro in the country used this rig, or said they did on TV and in magazines and books. If the Texas rig works as billed, why is it necessary to come up with dozens of weird shapes of worm hooks, such as the Messeler, the Tru-Turn, and the automatic .45? I rest my case for the time being. Whenever I want to fish a worm, I'll use the Bama Bug head or some other weedless hook—or rig the worm on an Aberdeen hook without any sort of weedless rig.

My digression about the nonweedless worm rig brings up a final point for this chapter. Because I went to a lot of trouble to design the Bama Bug with a weedguard doesn't mean that you should fish it that way. If you don't need the weedguard, snip it off. This is true of any weedguard lure. A weedguard is often helpful, and is sometimes quite necessary to fish a lure in the right places. But you will almost always hook more fish on any given lure if the weedguard is taken off. Play the odds. If hangups will be frequent when your lure is close to where the fish are, use a weedguard. If you're casting to schooling bass in the middle of the lake, use a lure without a weedguard. In defense of the weedguard, however, I'll have to say that some designs will prevent a bass or other head-shaking fish from throwing a lure once it's hooked.

Chapter 8

Designing Leadhead Jigs

The classic design of a jig—in which the hook eyelet comes out the top of the leadhead—gives the lure an action like no other. The center-weighted head, suitably dressed, is ideal for vertical fishing because, when properly worked, the jig darts about or swims like a minnow. The true center-weighted jig is built on a hook with a 90-degree leg.

Some jig hooks have a 60-degree leg, and others go down to 45 degrees or less. These are a better hooking design, but the bait doesn't hang minnowlike in the water. Jigs made on these hooks are suitable for fishing plastic worms and pork rinds along the bottom, and for most cast-and-retrieve fishing, but not for vertical fishing with a suspended lure. When fished on the bottom, these jigs, suitably dressed, resemble crawfish and other bottom creatures instead of swimming minnows. Further, they are usually (but not always) cast out and fished in at an angle to the bottom instead of being jigged vertically.

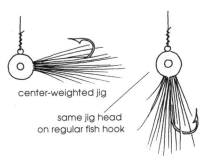

center-weighted jig

same jig head
on regular fish hook

Still other "jigs" are made on a straight hook, but these are not common and are usually reserved for straightforward cast-and-retrieve methods of fishing. I consider them to be weighted flies instead of jigs. Other lures, such as spoons, are sometimes called jigs, depending on how they are fished.

Although the classic jig design has a lot of advantages, it does have one fundamental shortcoming. The lure simply is not a good hooker, and I feel that fishing books and magazine articles and bass pros, pooping up the selling points of the latest kink in the jig-and-pork-rind fad, have ignored the problem.

Support for my position is not widespread. I haven't read all the angling literature, but at least one authority said some things that tend to support my belief. In *The New Standard Fishing Encyclopedia and International Angling Guide*, A. J. McClane wrote,

The first, and perhaps most vital, feature of a jig is the hook. On a lure of this type, a dull point just won't penetrate. Because of its hopping and diving action a jig is often struck by the fish when the hook is at a tangent to the direction of the rod. When jigging in deep water below a boat for instance, the hook bend instead of the point is facing the rod as the lure makes a free fall toward bottom. There is no reeling motion to start penetration such as you have when retrieving a plug through the water—a great percentage of the time. Furthermore, the jig is often grabbed by the fish when it's sitting perfectly still. Consequently, the point must be needle sharp. . . . A perfectly sharpened hook will "bite" no matter which way the fish hits.

I agree with the first part of McClane's statement, but I have to qualify the last comment about the "bite" of a sharp pointed hook. *If the sharp point touches meat, it will probably bite in, if the hook is set with some authority*; but, the way I see it, a large fish can engulf a small jig and, on the jerk, the jig's point (be it sharp or dull) doesn't touch meat. If the fish grabs the jig in the right spot—between the eyelet and the barb—it will probably be hooked. But if the whole works is engulfed, as bass are likely to do, the situation is less certain. The lack of what I call "effective bite" worries me.

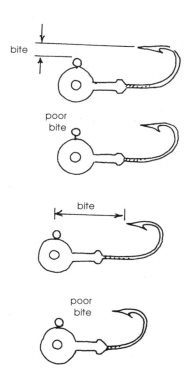

Because the hook eyelet sticks up in the way, jigs don't have the bite of a spoon or other lure. As the drawings show, the height of the eyelet as well as the length of the shank have a bearing on the jig's bite.

I hate to let go of this topic, but I don't know how to make it clearer. Perhaps I had better add that some writers have pointed out that small flies sometimes miss trout simply because the hook is too small to bite in. I might also add that the "effective bite" on most size 10 jig hooks is almost zero—and can be less than zero if the hook has a beak point. Think about it. Most of the jigs larger than size 6 will have enough point sticking up to bite in, but not always. Just a few days before this writing I saw some size 4 and size 2 crappie jigs made on a hook with a leg that stuck up about ½ inch above the plane of the point! It's hard to believe that any tackle firm, reputable or not, would put out such junk. It's even harder to believe that one of the largest chain stores in the United States would stock it.

JIG HOOKS

I'll jump right in with a hook design that I feel should be avoided in *any* jig. A lot of people prefer beak-point hooks and won't fish with anything else, although most of them don't know why. I think they associate them with the "Eagle Claw" idea, but maybe not. Philosophical fishermen who know their hooks insist that the beak point is best because it points toward the hook's eyelet, and therefore has a better line of pull. I allow that this could be a factor in a large hook that is difficult to stick, but it's simply of no consequence in a small hook. In any case, the "line of pull" theory simply doesn't apply to jigs, or doesn't work as billed.

My best advice is to avoid beak points altogether in smaller hooks, especially in jig hooks. If I could make a modest proposal: perhaps smaller jig hooks would work better with a reverse beak. At least such hooks would have a little more bite.

In any case, here are a few other topics to consider:

Shank. As a rule, longer-shanked jig hooks have more effective bite, and I prefer them for such fish as bass and crappie that have rather large mouths. With bluegill, however, longer-shank hooks make the lure more difficult for the fish to get into its mouth.

Base Material. Jig hooks are made with light wire as well as with heavier material. Generally, the lighter the wire, the easier it is to set the hook. The heavier hooks are usually larger in diameter, which makes them more difficult to stick into the fish. Heavy jig hooks fished on limber rods and light line are especially difficult to stick.

Finish. Jig hooks are available in several finishes, such as nickel plate, gold plate (or imitation gold plate), bronze, and so on. Some saltwater jig hooks are cadmium/tin plated. I normally use nickel-plated hooks for large jigs and gold Aberdeen hooks for small jigs. I have no particular reason for doing it this way, except that it's hard to stock all kinds of hooks.

Size. As a rule, the larger the jig hook the better the effective bite. But remember also that standard molds and jig-head weights will require pretty much standard hook sizes, although you can often go up one size or down one size, if desirable. But this may not always be advisable. On bluegill jigs, I think a size 6 hook is just too large. On a bass jig, it's almost always a good idea to go up one size, if possible. But remember that larger hooks are much more difficult to stick than smaller ones.

Leg Angle and Shank Length. Most jigs are molded on hooks with a 90-degree bend, and most molds are milled to take a hook with this bend. (Jig molds are available for 60-degree and other bends, too.) The better jig designs put the eye of the hook all the way down to the leadhead, and even into the head. This is mostly a matter of the length of the leg on the hook, but some molds won't accommodate a hook with a short leg because too much material is left between the mold cavity and the eyelet slot. This can be fixed, if necessary, by grinding out the slot to accommodate the hook eyelet. (See Chapter 9 for tips on modifying standard molds.)

Often the problem isn't with the mold but with the hook itself. On some of the smaller wire hooks, the leg may stick up too far because the longer legs work better in automatic production equipment. I can think of no other reason for making the leg so long. And, it's difficult for the do-it-yourselfer to do anything about the problem. Unbending and rebending the hooks won't work because the shank breaks at the bend. Using two pairs of needlenose pliers, I have bent a few light wire Aberdeen hooks into jig hooks to make a few lures to fish with, but it's slow going.

Recently I've seen pictures of small jig hooks that look better, at least in the catalogs, and perhaps the problem has been addressed. Even so, there are untold millions of jig hooks already on the market, and, to be honest, you don't always get what you see in a catalog.

LEADHEAD SHAPE

There must be a hundred different shapes for leadhead jigs, and if I tried to cover all of them here, new ones would probably be on the market before the book gets into print. Frankly, it doesn't matter very much in most cases, as long as the hook's eye comes out in more or less the center of mass. In other words, the jig should hang straight unless it's designed to be fished on bottom. Here are a few of the more common shapes.

Ball Jigs. These are the classic center-weighted jigs and require little explanation here. Commercial ball jigs and molds for do-it-yourselfers are available from tiny (1/32-ounce) to large (6-ounce); they're available with a collar, barb, or plain hook shank. The barb holds plastic grubs and similar attachments, and the collar serves as a skirt keeper. The plain hook model is usually chosen when hair or feathers are to be tied on. The plain hook isn't suitable for Living Rubber skirts, but works great for marabou and other feathers.

I like the center-weighted ball jig design very much—except for one thing. They're likely to hang up between rocks and in the crotch of two limbs—and they'll do a roll-over trick to make sure they get hung. For more on this, see the Livingston Roll-Over Test later in this chapter. Hangups notwithstanding, the action is good and the center-weighted ball-head design is quite popular.

Banana Jigs. These familiar jigs aren't quite center weighted and are more suited for cast-and-retrieve than for vertical fishing. They have no collar, and the dressing is usually tied onto the small part of the jig. I like these with a jig spinner. Like ball jigs and others with round bellies, these also roll over and hang badly on limbs and brush.

Arky Heads. I don't know where these jigs originated, but the first ones I saw were made with a monofilament weedguard and dressed with Living Rubber. My guess is that they came from the good state of Arkansas. In any case, they became pretty much standard (sometimes rigged with a Y-guard instead of a monofilament cluster) for the weedless jig and pork-rind baits. They are molded on 90-degree hooks, but with the eye forward so that it isn't a center-weighted rig. Although they are usually made with a weedguard and a collar-type skirt keeper, I have seen the head design used on

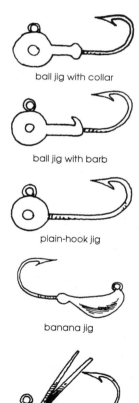

ball jig with collar

ball jig with barb

plain-hook jig

banana jig

Arky jig with
Y-guard

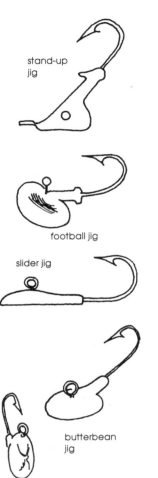

stand-up jig

football jig

slider jig

butterbean jig

shad dart

longnose jig

nonweedless jigs; I have also seen them rigged with wire weedguards. As often happens in the fishing business, similar names have been applied to similar heads, such as Sparkie and Arky.

Stand-up Jigs. These jigs, which have a flat bottom, or foot, are molded on a hook with a 45-degree bend and a regular eye (not a jig-hook eye). Theoretically, these sit on the bottom with the dressing sticking up enticingly at 45 degrees. They work fine in swimming pools and on other smooth bottoms. I like them rigged with floating-tail plastic worms.

Football Jigs. These weird-looking jigs are the shape of a football with a jig hook stuck through it sideways. They are popular for catching sauger on some parts of the Tennessee River, and as a rule are sparsely dressed. Since sauger are bottom fish, the idea behind the football design seems to be that it doesn't hang up as badly as a ball jig. Football jigs will certainly walk over limbs without turning 180 degrees.

Slider-Type Jigs. These thin jigs, flat on top and bottom, were developed to fish as a fall bait. Sometimes called "do-nothing jigs," they more or less fish themselves on the way down. Since these jigs have such a thin head, they would be ideal for a jig hook with a very short leg, if one were available. Try bending your own from an Aberdeen hook.

Butterbean Jigs. Just as the slider is designed with a flat bottom to make it sink slower and give it some action on the way down, another kind of jig is designed the other way so that it will sink quickly. Butterbean jigs are sometimes nice to have when fishing in very deep water.

Shad-Dart Jigs. This design, popular in some areas for shad fishing with spinning tackle, is shaped like a cone cut on a slant. Shad darts usually have no collar or barb, and are dressed with hair or feathers tied directly to the hook's shank. Shad darts, as you'd expect from the name, have more of a darting action on the retrieve than a ball jig.

Longnose Jigs. This design, often center weighted, is a very good one for swimming a curl-tail or plastic eel; the jig head continues the shape of the attachment. The long nose also helps them trip over limbs and rocks, making them a little less likely to hang up or wedge than most other jigs, including some with weedguards.

Shad Heads. Some time ago, soft-plastic shad-shaped attachments hit the market, based on a French lure made by the same outfit that came out with the first sickle-tailed grub, just before Mister Twister hit it big with a similar design. The shads had a good wiggle and of course caught fish. Before long, several variations were available, and several jig heads were developed to hold these plastic bodies. The problem is that the plastic bodies seldom match up with the heads.

shad-head jig, rigged and raw

Tube Jigs. These relatively new jigs are intended to be inserted into a soft-plastic tube that has an integral skirt. Thus, the leadhead is completely hidden and requires no paint or cleaning. It's a good design for crappie, white bass, and other fish that take swimming jigs. I expect to see more of these jigs in the future, and more types of plastic attachments are being developed for them. In fact, some people are already using this design for spinnerbaits and buzzbaits.

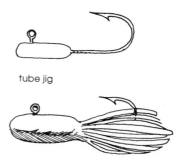

tube jig

JIGS WITH BLADES

There are several ways to fish spinnerbaits with jigs, and the jig-spinner attachment is by far the most popular, especially for light spinning. A number of brand-name lures, such as the Beetle Spin, use jig spinners, often dressed with with soft plastic. In addition to the popular baits, the jig-spinner forms are marketed in catalogs and those shops that deal with components. These are sometimes rigged with blades (usually smooth nickel Colorado), but not always. Three sizes of jig-spinner wires are marketed, and of course do-it-yourselfers can bend their own.

Another type, rather new, has a piece of wire molded into the head behind the jig-hook eyelet, as shown in the drawing. I don't recommend this design because it is not a good hooker and misses too many fish. These are called spin-jigs.

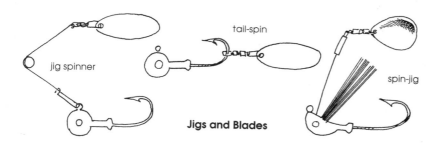

jig spinner

tail-spin

spin-jig

Jigs and Blades

Some people also rig a spinner blade onto the hook simply by first putting the blade onto a swivel or a snap swivel, then attaching the swivel to the jig hook (called a tail-spin), as shown in the middle drawing. Usually, surgical tubing is used, as when rigging a trailer hook.

WEEDLESS JIGS

Jigs have always caught bass, but they were never popular for these big-mouthed, cover-hugging fish until the weedless designs became available. These became "hot" a few years ago, especially when dressed with Living Rubber and tipped with pork rind. Fished on the bottom, they resemble crawfish but are likely to get hung up. There are several ways to make a jig more or less snagless or weedless.

fused end

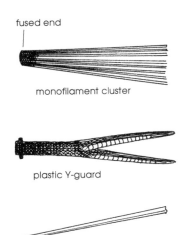

monofilament cluster

plastic Y-guard

wire guard

**Mold Inserts for
Making Weedless Jigs**

Wire Hook Guards. A pointed-nose rig called Sneaky Pete had the first wire guard I recall seeing on a jig. The wire came out the jig's front, folded over, and caught in a saddle shape just under the hook's barb. In other words, it worked exactly like the wire-guard weedless hooks. The next weedless jig I saw, manufactured by Four Rivers Tackle in Mississippi, used the same principle, but the wire came out the jig's body. Many molds can be modified to accept preformed wire, which can be purchased, or you can easily bend your own. I have always preferred this design over mono clusters and certainly Y-guard jigs. But I have to add that I am in the minority, and many bass pros wouldn't be caught dead with wire-guard worm hooks or jigs.

If you want to modify a mold to accommodate a wire guard, simply close it tightly, position it in a drill press, and drill a hole dead center on down to the cavity. The wire should go a good ways into the cavity so that it won't pull out easily, and the hole should go in straight, so that when the mold is opened the hole forms identical semicircles on each side. The angle of hole in relation to the hook's barb isn't too important because the wire can be bent over later to saddle under the hook's barb. Actually, I prefer to go a little further with this rig, and put a dogleg in the wire. This makes a guard that isn't as easily "sprung" while the fish mouths the bait, but it's easier to set when the angler jerks on the rod. The same idea can be used on wire-guard weedless hooks.

Monofilament Clusters. Clusters of hard, heat-resistant monofilament are inserted into the mold before the lead is poured. The hot lead fuses them together, and they stay in place nicely. Of course, the mold must have a slot on each side to accommodate the monofilament; this should be, but often isn't, at the right angle.

These weedguards can be used on several kinds of jigs, including ball and banana, but are more often used on the bottom-scooters that are so popular for bass fishing.

One problem is that the clusters are fused on one end and the other end is apparently cut with a hot wire. This in turn can fray the ends badly, causing them to tangle together to such an extent that they prevent the hook's point from sticking into the fish. This problem can sometimes be helped by rubbing the ends briskly between the fingers, or by cutting the strands with snippers instead of with a hot wire. The snippers are slow, however, and impede production to such an extent that this technique is unlikely to be used in mass production. Do-it-yourselfers, however, can take more time with weedguards.

Another problem is that most of the weedguards are too long, and should, I think, be cut so that they bend down without quite touching the hook. Longer clusters are needed to facilitate speedy pouring, however, so manufacturers tend to leave them long, whereas fishermen need them short. I always cut off the end after the jig has been poured and painted. Cutting the cluster to clear the hook usually cures the end matting problem dis-

cutting off the top
of the weedguard
will often help
alleviate matting

cussed above, so that two birds can be killed with one stone.

Still another problem is that the monofilament cluster greatly complicates the painting of the jig. Those weedguards that are dipped will surely clog up with paint, and the monofilament cluster will become so stiff that it won't bend, which prevents the hook from setting. When I was in the lure business, we sprayed our jigs—and took the trouble to insert a straw over each cluster to keep the paint away. It works, and the monofilament bent all the way down to the head, giving the jig much better hooking properties. But most manufacturers are not going to do this, especially if they have to watch every penny in order to compete in the discount stores.

In any case, clusters that are clogged with paint can be unclogged by separating the strands and working them back and forth.

Still another problem is that some of the weedguard clusters are inserted at too steep an angle, which is determined by the mold. This came about, no doubt, because weedguards, set at 45 degrees made it difficult to tie on Living Rubber and other dressings. In any case, the only sensible thing you can do with such a jig is to cut off the weedguard—or throw the whole thing away. But don't throw away the mold. Modify it with a rat-tail file, making a slot at a better angle, as discussed in Chapter 9.

Y-Guard Jigs. Some years ago, I reasoned that the angling world would welcome a better way to rig a worm. The old weedless hook wasn't too well accepted, and, as I knew, the Texas rig missed too many strikes. I came up with a weedless hook that used two prongs of stiff monofilament—but not *too* stiff. I used a keel hook (which wasn't ideal, but it was the best I could do at the time) and hand-tied monofilament prongs. I wanted a little weight on the rig, and I designed a leadhead with the right slope to give the mono prongs the right angle. Then I decided to wrap a Latex thorax onto the hook, and to add a tuft of hair.

Well, the Bass Nymph-O worked better, for me, than any worm rig I had ever used, and was very, very good for fishing in grass. We made a few thousand, and I was surprised to find that bass anglers didn't jump all over the thing; I thought the merits of the design were self-evident. But it was hard to make, and therefore expensive. Quality control was also something of a problem, so I think it was probably doomed from the start. Lew Childre (the famous bass tackle manufacturer) told me that truth. He thought it was a great worm rig—but he said that I wasn't going to change the way people fish.

Several people in the tackle industry saw the rig, however, and I think it influenced the development of the two-prong weedguard. About a year after I put out some of the lures, I went to a large tackle show in Kansas City as a member of the press. (At the time, I was publishing *Bass Fishing News*, a tabloid for tournament anglers.) At a booth I saw a new jig—at least new to me—that was being manufactured by a fellow of my acquaintance. He seemed a little embarrassed when I took notice of the jig design, and I believe until this day that he got the idea from the Bass Nymph-O.

In any case, this was the first of the Y-guard jigs I had seen. I was look-

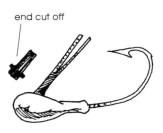

end cut off

V-guard jig

ing them over carefully, testing the weedguard with my finger, when the owner asked, "What do you think, A. D.?"

"The weedguard's too stiff," I said.

"No hell it ain't!" he said. "These things catch bass. This I guarantee."

Sure, they catch bass. But they'd catch more with a better weedguard. I dropped the subject, but I also wanted to tell him that the "post," or round part, was not only too long but also too stiff. The two prongs were limber enough, but they were too close together. They were also too wide, or flat, causing the guard to hit the hook when depressed at a slight angle. I didn't understand why these weren't perfectly round, and I still don't understand the thinking of whoever designed them. The length of the overall guard probably had something to do with inserting the Y-guard into the mold during production, but, still, I feel that a better design would have been to have a post-and-prong arrangement that bent all the way down to the leadhead. In any case, the drawing shows a typical Y-guard and a sketch of how the do-it-yourselfer can modify these. Of course, you may also have to modify the mold accordingly.

In any event, the popularity of these jigs has faded somewhat, no doubt because they simply miss too many fish. These guards are still available, however, in several sizes and colors. Molds designed to accept Y-guards are also readily available.

V-Guard Jigs. As I said earlier, the first monofilament V-guard I ever saw was on the Bass Nymph-O. This wasn't a true jig, however, and had some serious problems in hook design as well as in manufacture. Clearly, a true V-guard jig was needed. The problem was that both prongs of the V would have to go some ways into the leadhead in order to be molded in, and this would require a three-piece mold, which is difficult to make and requires much more production time to turn out the jigs, which shoots up the price of the completed product. It can be done, however, and David Livingston at Sunkeye Heads came out with the first one I ever saw. It has a hinged mold with a hole in the top, half on either side. A plug (with a handle on it) goes into the hole, and the monofilament prongs go into channels on either side of the plug. The procedure goes like this: (1) the jig hook is put into the mold as usual; (2) the mold is closed as usual; (3) the plug is put in place; (4) the monofilament prongs are inserted in the hole on either side of the plug, all the way into the leadhead; (5) the lead is poured into the mold as usual; (6) the plug is removed; and (7) the mold is opened and the V-guard jig is removed.

There may be other ways of making the V-guard, and some such jigs that I know about were made by drilling into the leadhead and then gluing in the mono prongs with Super Glue. The problem here is in getting the holes in at exactly the right angle. In my opinion, the three-piece mold is by far the best way to go, but a mold of this sort is not on the market and may never be. If you're handy with tools, you can make your own.

A MODEST PROPOSAL

When plugging the upper reaches of the Choctawhatchee River in Alabama years ago, my fishing buddies and I had a rule that you had to catch fish in order to eat fish. Once you got away from the bridges, the banks were thick with brush and the stream was cluttered with felled trees and treetops. Working the stream with a jonboat was all but impossible because many logs blocked the way. Obviously, accurate casting was important. It was more necessary back then because we usually had only one or two lures, or minnows, as we called them, and they were rigged with at least two sets of treble hooks. Of course, we preferred floating/diving minnows simply because if we did break one off it would sometimes resurface and we could chase it downstream. I might add that we fished with old bait-casting reels in which the pawl and worm gear worked during the cast, and even the handle turned. Backlashes were common, and these made it even more important to cast a floating lure. If any of us had cast a leadhead jig into the East Choctawhatchee, he would have been considered crazy.

I've always wanted to get Homer Circle, the Angling Editor of *Sports Afield,* to participate in such a fishing trip on the East Choctawhatchee, anywhere above Adam's Mill. More than once he has said, in print, that if he had to have one lure for survival purposes, it would surely be a jig. One jig on the Choctawhatchee? Well, Homer knows more than I do about fishing, but, to shift the odds further in my favor, I would take him to the Bedsprings Hole, which is on private property owned by a friend of mine. My friend doesn't fish and got tired of worm cans and potato chip bags being left along the banks of the hole. Finally, he threw several sets of bedsprings into the water, thereby making it strictly a topwater plug hole. After the bedsprings, he cut the timber on both sides of the river, letting the tops and limbs fall where they may. In short, I'll lay even money to Homer, or to any gambling man, that if they cast a leadhead into this stretch of river and count to three before they start the retrieve, they'll never see the jig again, unless they're willing to get their ass wet.

Except for the Little George and other tailspinners, I would be hard put to design a better lure than a ball jig for hanging up on limbs. Indeed, it's almost impossible to get a ball jig or a banana jig through a treetop. If you don't believe this, try the Livingston roll test. First, tie a size 2/0 ball jig onto a string. Hold the string in your right hand. Stick out your left index finger. Slowly pull the jig over your extended finger. As it comes across your finger, it will turn, flip over, and catch on the hook. It'll do it every time. It'll do the same thing on a limb in the water.

Further, it will hang in the crotch or between rocks and riprap. What happens, of course, is that the leadhead drops down in a hole or otherwise gets between two rocks and cuts off, fast. I know some tailwaters that are, in low water, almost as bad as the bedspring hole on the Choctawhatchee.

Weedless jigs, with fiber guards or Y-guards, really don't help much in rocks and aren't foolproof in brush. Fishing a jig with a flat-bottomed nose, such as the shad-dart design, will help somewhat when you pull it over a limb, but it won't help very much. Dan Gapen and no doubt others have designed jigs in one shape or another, to get away from the rounded bottom of a ball or banana jig, but then have not been entirely successful in convincing the millions of American anglers that there is a better way. The plain truth is that a hunk of lead attached to a line is going to hang on something, especially if it is bounced along the bottom.

I have gone into some detail on this matter of hanging jigs in order to address another problem without getting laughed out of the country. Since the jig is going to hang anyway, we might as well start thinking about a jig that will hook more fish.

FINAL ADVICE

In my opinion, how a jig is to be dressed and fished has a bearing on the design to choose. With open-water jigs, the hooking problem should receive lots of attention. When you are bumping or scooting the jig along the bottom, the weedless factor should receive lots of attention. It's easy to make a jig where the point of the hook is protected, but you don't want it to be fishless. My advice is: (1) always have the weedguard short enough to clear the hook's point, and (2) use a limber weedguard, and one that bends all the way down to the leadhead. When considering the second point, remember that the jig will be in water, and will therefore "weigh" much less than it does in the air. In short, it won't take much strength in the weedguard to deflect it from brush, especially on a slow retrieve. Usually, all you need is enough guard to protect the hook on the "roll over." This philosophy will surely cost you a few jigs—but it will save you some fish.

ordinary ball jig

I might add that I have successfully fished jigs on the bottom without any weedguard at all. The trick is to use heavy Living Rubber (which I call spider rubber) tied so that it sticks out like legs, protecting the hook a little on the rollover. I might add that a white spider skirt sporting a tuft of red marabou and trailed by a pork lizard or other long pork rind is a deadly combination on largemouth bass.

Any time you're missing fish on a small jig, size 8 or 10, you might try bending the hook point up quite a bit. Or, if you want to shock everybody, you might bend the hook around 180 degrees. Such an upside-down jig will have a crazy line of pull for fishing deep or for vertical jigging and isn't recommended for this purpose, but it may surprise you when you are casting and reeling small jigs rather fast, as when fishing for schooling white bass.

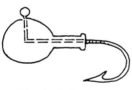

Livingston's shocker

Such jigs also pass Livingston's Roll Test and may, in fact, be more snagless than regular ball jigs. I don't really expect anybody to fish with upside-down jigs, but if the idea causes you to think about your hook's ability to stick fish, then the words won't have been wasted.

Working with Lead and Molds

A few years ago, melting and molding lead was, I suspect, something of a fascination for many boys who loved to fish. It was for me. I remember melting it in jar lids, sitting by the hot wood fire on cold winter nights. If the lids were crimped just right, a lip was formed that helped direct the lead when it was poured into a crude mold. Of course, the lid was held somewhat precariously by the rim with pliers. Vise-Grips would have been nice, but they were unavailable back then. Mostly, I made large "set hook" sinkers, which were poured into holes drilled into two pieces of hard wood clamped together. A slim, smooth nail (or pull pin) in the center formed a hole for the fishing line.

Modern do-it-yourselfers have much better equipment, but the principle is the same: lead is melted and poured into a mold of one sort or another. Although a cast-iron ladle can be used for melting as well as for pouring lead, modern do-it-yourselfers can purchase an electrically heated hand-held melting and pouring pot. These work fairly well, but the lead tends to spill out and, of course, small molds tend to fill too quickly and overflow, thereby causing the lead to run down the sides. Obviously, pouring lead from any sort of ladle or other hand-held device can be dangerous and messy. Fortunately, there is a better tool for most applications.

Hilt's electric lead melter and ladle

The electrically heated lead pot with a spout in the bottom is by far the best way to melt and pour lead on a small scale, at least for small lures. These pots have a lever-operated plunger valve that releases a spurt of lead directly into the mold when it's opened. If the lever is held up, a steady stream of lead pours out. If it's opened and shut very quickly, only a short stream comes out. If it's held open longer, a longer stream comes out. The operator can easily control the flow.

Several of these pots are on the market, listed in catalogs for luremakers as well as for hobbyists who pour lead bullets. The most common model holds 10 pounds of lead, which is satisfactory for most uses. Anyone who

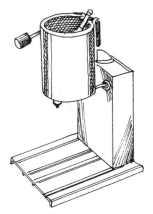

Lee 10-pound lead pot

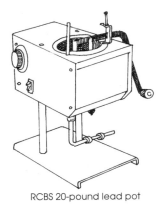

RCBS 20-pound lead pot

does lots of pouring, however, should look at the 20-pound pots.

All of the electric pots have adjustable temperature controls (I have also seen a larger gas-heated production pot that worked the same way), and these are very, very important. It's best to follow the directions for the particular pot, but remember that different alloys behave differently and that one mold is not like another. It is therefore entirely possible to pour one spinnerbait perfectly at a certain temperature, but a buzzbait of the same size might not pour at all. That is, the lead won't fill out the cavity and the head will be a reject. Sometimes the imperfection will be small, and sometimes it will be blatant. This can be quite frustrating, and sometimes there seems to be no reason for failure.

I might add here that pouring egg sinkers is a snap compared with pouring spinnerbaits and buzzbaits. With sinkers, rejects present no problem except for wasted time and electrical energy used to heat the lead. Rejected sinkers are merely dropped back into the pot, remelted, and cast again. With spinnerbaits and buzzbaits, however, you have a hook and a piece of wire to salvage. A luremaker who works for profit will tell you that half a day's work can be lost while trying to get a rig to pour, resulting in hundreds of rejected pieces. If they are put back into the pot, the wire and hook discolor and distemper. If he throws the wire and hook away, he loses money. If he tries to melt the lead without immersing the hook and wire, he wastes lots of time. Consequently, anyone who earns money with a lead pot will be interested in getting things right. But there are so many variables that it's hard to pinpoint what's wrong.

For one thing, there are vast differences in "lead," and rarely will the do-it-yourselfer find wheel weights or scrap lead that will do everything he needs to do. The so-called plumbers lead, sometimes available in 5-pound ingots from supply houses, is usually the best bet for the do-it-yourselfer. As a rule, scrap lead is very unpredictable and wheel weights are seldom satisfactory for spinnerbaits and buzzbaits, although they might work for some sinkers and large jigs. My advice for the spinnerbait man is to get rid of a batch of lead that doesn't work, perhaps pouring it into weights for duck decoys, anchors, and so on.

I have known people who purchased 25-pound bags of lead shot for making spinnerbaits and other lures. This isn't a bad way to go if you find exactly what you want. When you do find it, stick with one manufacturer and one size shot. That's right. Lead for shot is an exact alloy specified by the ammunition manufacturer and blended at the lead plant. What works for #4 shot might not work for a #9. Arsenic is present in most alloys and tends to make lead ball up (like mercury), and it is therefore a desirable element to have when making shot for shells. Such shot is made by pouring molten lead through a screen of suitable mesh.

If the hobbyist has a batch of lead that won't pour, perhaps the lead is "balling up" too badly because it contains too much arsenic. Antimony, on the other hand, does the opposite from arsenic, tending to make the lead run and string out. If a particular batch of lead tends to flash badly, it might well have too much antimony in it. But the hobbyist doesn't have much control over this sort of thing, and the best he can do is realize that the alloy can cause his rig not to pour some baits properly. He should also know that a batch of lead that won't work for ⅛-ounce buzzbaits might work just fine for ½-ounce spinnerbaits. So, several batches of lead may be in order for the complete do-it-yourselfer.

text continued on page 82

SAFETY

Most people realize these days that lead can poison your system, and there have been many horror stories in the media about problems with lead paint and lead plumbing. Even fine crystal containing lead has come under fire, and I remember that years ago a friend of mine came to the conclusion that the Roman Empire declined and fell because the aristocracy drank too much wine from lead goblets. In any case, it has been well established that lead can be harmful to humans, and, as modern hunters know, to ducks. For this reason, anyone who works with leadheads should be very careful, and should wash his hands frequently and especially before eating, if he eats with his fingers. Anyone who eats Finger Lickin' Good Chicken while cleaning leadheads is asking for trouble.

But remember that as a rule it is the cleaning and handling of raw (unpainted) leadheads (and sprues) that cause problems. Many people can pour a thousand spinnerbait or buzzbait heads without even touching the lead, especially if the lead is put into the pot with the aid of pliers or tongs. Consider the pouring process: the operator puts the hook and wire into the mold, closes it, holds it under the lead pot, hits the lever, takes the mold out, opens it, and removes the hot piece by the wire or hook. He simply doesn't touch the hot lead. Lead is usually touched when the sprue is removed, when the *head* is cleaned, and, often, when the head is mounted for painting.

The fumes that rise from the top of the lead pot may be a hazard for anyone who pours lots of lead. It's difficult to say what exactly is in these fumes, especially when using scrap lead. The best bet is to use a pot only in a well-ventilated area, and make sure you're sitting upwind. For example, if you sit at a table you can have a window open at your back and an exhaust fan ahead of you, so that the air flow takes the fumes away from you.

Melted lead can also cause burns, and lead pots can be dangerous. They aren't likely to tip over, but, to prevent a molten application of Murphy's Law, they can be easily clamped or bolted to a work table. In any case, you shouldn't have a pot full of molten lead when children are playing in the area, or where good

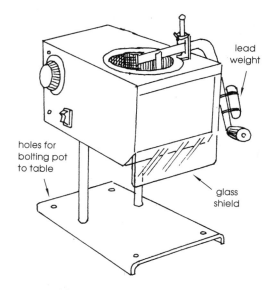

lead weight

holes for bolting pot to table

glass shield

Modified 20-Pound Lead Pot

ol' boys might start wrestling around. It's a good idea to put a lid over your lead pot, and one of these can be made rather easily from a sheet of aluminum with the aid of a saw. Such a cover will help hold the heat in the pot, and to some extent will help control the fumes. If you intend to pour a large number of lures, remember to keep a few bars of lead on top of the cover so that they will be warm when you put them into the pot. This will reduce melting time and save energy.

Lead spills and spatters will happen from time to time, and some manufacturers might recommend that heavy, long-sleeved gloves be worn during the casting process. These will be all right for anyone pouring large sinkers, but not for pouring lures with hooks and wire in them, simply because the gloves slow down the work. Most people will pour without the gloves, and they will be burned from time to time. Of course, most of these burns will be minor. To protect the eyes, consider wearing goggles or protective glasses. If you pour lots of lead with a rather large pot, you might also consider installing a splash window with a sheet of glass. This will give quite a lot of protection, while at the same time allowing you to watch what you're doing while fitting the mold to the spout. Again, I owe David Livingston for this idea.

Anyone who is serious about making leadheads on a production basis is, of course, advised to locate a lead plant that will work with him. As a rule, these people will want to sell in very large quantities, but you may be able to get smaller amounts. Even so, this lead will often be in 70-pound pigs, and you must be able to melt this down (or otherwise reduce it) to smaller portions. At Sunkeye, David Livingston heats up a cast-iron pot large enough to melt three 70-pound pigs, and dips the molted lead out with a ladle. He pours it into cast-iron corn-stick pans. These elongated pieces weigh about a pound and handle easily with split-ring pliers, which permits the operator to pick up a piece of lead by one end and ease it down into the lead pot without a splash. Split-ring pliers, I might add, have a tooth on the end that bites into the piece of lead, giving a firm grip. Obviously, you don't want a 1-pound chunk of lead to slip while your hand is near the top of the pot.

Perhaps I had better add here that a bottom-spouted lead pot can be used in two ways. First, the mold can be held under the spout and some distance below it, so that a stream of lead is visible when the lever is operated. People who use molds and pots in this manner usually want some sort of rest to hold the mold the same distance from the pot on each pour. Some pots have a built-in guide. This method may work for large lures and large sinkers, but for small stuff the cavity and gate fill up quickly and overflow, making a mess on the sides of the mold and on the work table. At least this has been my experience. It also creates lots of lead sprue to be remelted. A better way, at least for spinnerbaits, buzzbaits, and most medium-size jigs with weedguard material, is to fit the pot's pouring spout into the gate of the mold. If these fit together nicely—as well they should—then overruns and

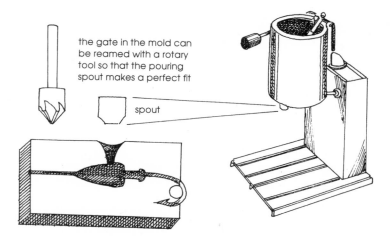

the gate in the mold can be reamed with a rotary tool so that the pouring spout makes a perfect fit

spout

spills are not as likely to occur. Further, if the fit is so good that they actually seal, then you have pressure working for you to fill out the mold instead of merely free-falling lead. Also, the sprue is not as large.

If the pot's spout doesn't fit into the mold's gate, take a look at some reaming tools for a drill press or hand drill. If you can find a tool with the right angle, you can quickly ream out the gate to accommodate the spout. It's best to chuck the mold in a drill press and proceed carefully; you don't want to enlarge the gate too much, and you should take extra care not to enlarge the opening into the lure cavity. If you do, you'll have large sprues that will be difficult to remove and heads that are hard to clean before painting.

In any case, I highly recommend that you try this method. Although it can cause some problems (as discussed in the troubleshooting section later in this chapter), I feel that it's by far the best way to pour most leadheads.

TYPES OF MOLDS

I've seen some mold-making kits on the market that were designed to enable a hobbyist to duplicate a leadhead. Essentially, they involve suspending the leadhead in a suitable plastic box and pouring, or molding, a plastic mix all around it. The plastic is soft, and when it sets it has to be cut in half. Obviously, the cut must be exact if the two halves of the new mold are to work properly. If it isn't cut precisely, how are you going to insert the hook and wire? In any case, after you get two halves, you have to cut a gate for the lead and you have to devise a way of holding the two halves together.

We made the old Bass Nymph-O with such a system, although we poured half the mold in a plastic hook box, then pressed the lure plug into it, let it set, and applied a very light coating of Vaseline or some such lubricant. (If you want to try this method, it's best to experiment to find a suitable nonstick surface. With some modern formulas, perhaps no coating at all is needed. Or you might try pouring the bottom half plain and then adding a touch of color to the top half, thereby making a two-toned division, which in turn will help you in cutting the mold halves. In any case, if you buy into such a rig, read the manufacturer's instructions carefully. Then gamble with modifications if you have to.) Anyhow, the Nymph-O mold worked pretty well for a while. Then the heads started to get larger and larger, and were not perfectly shaped. I think that the heat of the lead causes the plastic to lose its shape. Maybe a low-melt alloy would work better than lead and give the molds a longer life.

In any case, aluminum molds work better than plastic and in recent years a great variety of molds of good quality have become available. These are inexpensive and are often easy to modify. It's also possible to have metal molds custom made to your specifications. If you can provide a "plug," or sample, several firms can make a mold for you at a reasonable price. (Check the sources listed in the Appendix.)

It's also possible to buy blank molds, complete with handles, that can be machined to your specifications by a local machinist, although I don't recommend this. Such work can be very expensive and in the end the mold may not be what you want or need, either because the machinist didn't deliver, or misunderstood what you wanted, or he thought it would work better another way. Remember that the two halves of the mold must be machined perfectly, provisions must be made for wire and hooks to be inserted, the mold must have a gate that can be reached easily for pouring the lead, and then the halves must fit together perfectly. It can be done, but, as I said, I wouldn't recommend this method.

It would be better to locate a firm that specializes in fishing molds. Usually, such firms are experienced in the placement of gates, wire slots, and so on, in addition to being expert in forming a precise cavity for the lure body. They will also know the kind of materials to use, and may have standard blocks on hand, whereas other machinists may have to spend a good deal of time determining what to use and where to get it. (Some of these moldmakers are listed in the Appendix, and from time to time one advertises in the classified pages of *Fishing Tackle Trade News* or *Fishing Tackle Retailer*.)

When I first went into the lure business, we paid to have a few molds custom made for us. These worked pretty well for making a few samples, but they were not quite what we wanted. For one thing, we had a little trouble in making all sizes look like the others in profile. Since we had four sizes of spinnerbaits and three sizes of buzzbaits, we could see that getting a perfectly matched set could be quite expensive. So we decided that we had to make our own molds. David Livingston was to be in charge of pouring all the leadheads, and, being innovative and good with hand tools, he set out to make his own molds. First he made a plug or spinnerbait head in all sizes and another similar plug for all sizes of the buzzbaits. Then he poured a layer of fiberglass into a plastic hook box and fitted the plug into it, going halfway up. When this hardened, he applied a little parting compound and then poured more fiberglass into the box. When it set, he removed the two halves and took out the plug. Now he had plugs for a mold.

The fiberglass plugs were then used to sand-cast aluminum molds. First he tried this method with the aid of a local foundry, but the resulting "mold" was far too imprecise to be usable. Further, this was for only one head size—and we needed seven. So he set out to do his own sand casting, which involved melting aluminum, which he did with the aid of gas heat, air pressure, and a cast-iron pot. After finally melting the aluminum, he dipped it with a long-handled ladle and poured it into his sand-casting set. When things cooled off, we broke open the sand expecting to find shiny new mold blocks, but we were sorely disappointed. The "mold" halves looked more like ears than squared-up mold blocks. I quickly began to have doubts, but David stuck with the process and finally poured some molds we could use. He did, however, have to finish them by hand, which he had expected to do, using a set of dental tools.

He also sand-cast some handles to hold the mold plugs, and these were put together without hinges. The nice thing about this system is that everything was so adjustable. One handle fit into another by inserting a slot under a screw, which was adjustable. Then the mold halves were drilled and attached to the handle with bolts in such a way that the alignment was adjustable. One size handle held all the mold blocks.

Some people who read this will laugh, thinking that there are better and faster ways of making leadheads. But the fact is that David's homemade molds produce the most consistent leadheads I have seen in the entire tackle industry, lure after lure, batch after batch, year after year. In short, he has made a million heads, and he won't even consider using a multicavity mold and certainly not a centrifugal mold. It's hard enough, he says, to get one cavity to fill out right.

In any case, there are some fairly good single-cavity molds on the market. If these aren't quite what you want, they can sometimes be modified or customized to suit your needs or fancy. The point that I want to make here is that you shouldn't discount a single-cavity mold, either for making a few baits for your own use or to make some for sale.

It's true that some commercial molds will accommodate several spinnerbaits or buzzbaits at one time. Even so, it's best to use only one cavity at a time (whichever one works better and is easier to fit to or hold under the lead pot's pouring spout). Remember that rejects contain hooks and wire; with a single-cavity mold you have only one reject at a time. Also, a good single-cavity mold is just as fast, if not faster, than a multicavity mold. After

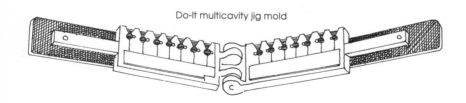

Do-It multicavity jig mold

all, you've got to lay in each wire and hook individually, you've got to pour the lead into each gate, and you've got to remove each leadhead after pouring.

I must point out, though, that small jigs without weedguards pour successfully and faster in multicavity molds. Also, I must add that many of the jigs, spinnerbaits, and buzzbaits on the market are made by centrifugal casting, discussed briefly under a separate heading at the end of this chapter.

ELEMENTS OF MOLDS

Whatever kind of mold you use, all have common elements that have a bearing on how well they work for making leadheads. The various parts are shown in the drawing, and are discussed below.

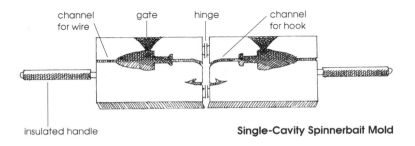

Single-Cavity Spinnerbait Mold

Gate. The size of the gate determines how well a mold performs. As a rule, the larger the gate the better it pours. The moldmaker therefore leans toward a large gate so that his molds will work nicely from the word go. A large gate, however, makes a large sprue, which is usually removed before painting. Obviously, a small-diameter sprue (or at least smaller at the point where the gate enters into the lure cavity) is easier to remove than a large one. A small sprue is also much easier to clean. Thus, the operator who wants high-volume production will prefer a small gate.

In any case, remember that gates can be made larger if the operator suspects that they need to be larger in order to pour. Normally this is best accomplished by working on either side of the mold with a rat-tail file. Remember, however, that it is almost impossible to make a large gate smaller, so that anyone filing on a mold should proceed carefully.

If you make your own molds, or choose to have them custom made, consider starting with a small gate and then enlarging it as needed. If your moldmaker argues, tell him four or five times that you want to start with a small gate opening so that you won't have a large sprue, and that you won't hold it against him if the mold doesn't work perfectly on the first try.

Gate placement is sometimes a problem, and I usually want mine under the belly of the leadhead simply because that's where they work best, as a rule, and because that's where they fit best in spinnerbait and buzzbait molds, where you've got a hook on one and a long wire on the other. On some designs, the wire also doglegs over the mold, so that gating from the bottom is the only practical way to go.

From a cleaning or painting point of view, it would be better to have the gate at the end of the skirt keeper, so that the skirt would cover up any blemish made by removing the sprue, but this design causes some problems in pouring, partly because the lead must flow farther from one end to the other and partly, I suspect, because air rushing from the larger part of the cavity as the lead is poured causes blow holes and other problems. The best design has the gate going into the largest part of the cavity. When inverted, this will also be the highest point in the mold; air won't cause as much of a problem as it would in the small skirt-keeper cavity. The gate could, of course, be run into the top part of the lure, but usually the wire or weedguard material gets in the way, leaving the bottom about the only place for it. Of course, the gate should not be longer than necessary simply because you don't want to have a long sprue.

Insert Slots. Most lure molds are made with channels to accommodate hooks, wire, and weedguards. On commercial molds, these are put in at the factory—but they aren't always in the right place and may not be the right size. Often a mold will be available with or without such slots. For example, you can buy a ⅜-ounce mold for making weedless fiber-guard jigs. These are fine if the weedguard is where you want it. If not, you can buy the same head mold without the weedless feature, then work out your own channel. Start by marking one side of the mold very carefully with a scribe and a straightedge. With a dental tool, or other such sharp-pointed tool, scrape out a little metal from one end to the other. (This is easy to do on most aluminum molds, as the material is quite soft.) Next, lightly coat the scribed side of the mold with a substance called Persian blue. (If you can't locate this stuff, consult with a local machinist.) Then close and open the mold. Some of the Persian blue will have rubbed off on the blank side of the mold, clearly showing where the channel should be. You now have the angle for making the channel on either side of the mold. From then on, it's file and check until you have an opening large enough to accommodate the weedguard. Usually, the slots for the fiber guard are larger in diameter on one end, where the material is inserted into the closed mold. Then it tapers down to the exact size where the material enters the cavity.

Channels for wire and for hooks can be made in pretty much the same

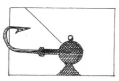

carefully scribe a line
for weedguard angle

form a channel for
a small piece of wire

enlarge cavity with
rat-tail file

way. First scribe a line, then work it out by scraping with some sort of hand tool. The job can be finished by sawing off the eye of a hook and using the shank as a finishing tool.

Hook-Eyelet Slot. You can also modify the slots for hook eyelets by either scraping away some of the material or perhaps using a drill bit of the proper size. In the sketch at left, note that the original eyelet slot was made for jig hooks that have a long eyelet leg. It will not accept a short-legged hook. The modification will accept either.

Eyes. Few of the molds on the market have built-in eyes, which are very, very helpful during the painting process. These built-in eyes are easy to make, if you have a drill press. (A hand-held drill can be used, but a drill press is highly recommended unless you want cross-eyed lure heads.) The easiest to make is a bugeye. Simply drill partly into the mold, so that the drill bit makes a conical depression in the aluminum, as shown in the drawing. A depression in the aluminum makes a bugeye, or frog eye, on the lure head. These help locate the spot for the paint, but are not ideal since they are difficult to paint.

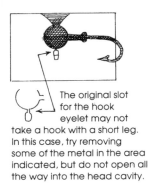

The original slot for the hook eyelet may not take a hook with a short leg. In this case, try removing some of the metal in the area indicated, but do not open all the way into the head cavity.

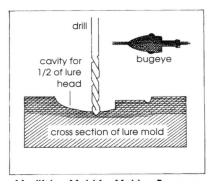

Modifying Mold for Making Bugeyes

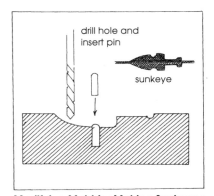

Modifying Mold for Making Sunkeyes

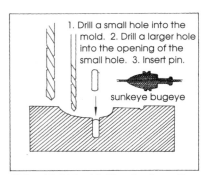

1. Drill a small hole into the mold. 2. Drill a larger hole into the opening of the small hole. 3. Insert pin.

Modifying Mold for Making Sunkeye Bugeyes

A sunken eye works better for the painter, but it's a little more difficult to achieve. First, a hole must be drilled into either side of the mold in the exact spot, then pins are rounded off and tapped into the holes. These pins must fit perfectly so that they'll stay in place. The advantage of the sunkeye, of course, is that a small droplet of paint can be applied without it running out of the cavity.

If you like the bugeye effect, but want the convenience of the sunken eye, combine the methods. Drill out the bugeyes, then drill a hole and insert the pin, as shown, in the bugeye hole.

Handles. Most small molds have handles. In addition to providing a relatively cool grip, the handles are used to hold the mold halves together, under slight pressure, during the pouring process, and also help to separate the mold halves after pouring. Often, round metal rod handles are fitted into holes in the mold halves, then covered with rubber or plastic to improve the grip and provide insulation. Other molds, such as the

Do-It series, have wooden handles attached to the mold halves.

The need for adequate handles is obvious, but the angler who wants to pour a few baits to fish with can get by with mold halves held together by clamps. They should never be held by hand, however, because of the possibility of hot lead overflowing and causing serious burns. People who make lures for profit will of course want a handle that is comfortable as well as safe to use.

Stops and Guides. These devices are not normally seen on molds, but they are, or can be, a great help for keeping hook and wire aligned. Remember that the hook and wire, when viewed from the top, ought to be in the same line, and neither should be cocked to left or right. Usually, the wire of a spinnerbait or buzzbait sticks out the top of the mold and can hang a little one way or the other. Precise alignment can be achieved by attaching an arm or guide of some sort to the mold, so that the wire is kept in one place. A machine screw can be installed at an appropriate spot so that the wire can be held in place under tension. Alternatively, a small magnet (as from a kitchen cabinet latch), can be installed on the arm to hold the wire.

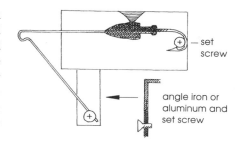

— set screw

angle iron or aluminum and set screw

Sometimes hooks are free to move about in a mold, and getting them down in the right spot can be a problem—as can keeping them there. Within a head, a hook eye can be almost at the nose, at the skirt keeper, or anywhere in between. The center is usually the best spot. I recommend installing some sort of stop (such as the set screw shown in the sketch), then using it as a guide for properly spacing everything. That way, each head will look alike and you'll always have the right-length wire and hook. Remember that putting the connection toward the front of the cavity will make the "wire" longer and the "hook" shorter. In my opinion, you need all the hook you can get. Such a hook stop helps in several ways. First, it gives the operator something to "hang" everything on. Consider the process. The operator opens the mold. Then he inserts the wire into the eye of the hook. Then he puts the hook's bend down over the post. Holding things tight, he lays the entire assembly down. Then he rests the wire in place, hopefully under slight tension, so that everything stays in place until he gets the mold shut. Neat.

Admittedly, such modifications take some time, but they will pay off in the long run if you intend to make lots of lures. Besides, it's fun to make things work better.

I knew of one outfit in Georgia that had a problem with spinnerbait hook and wire alignment. They made a jig and soldered the hook and wire together so that it would go into the mold in one piece. If you try this method, remember that everything will have to be lined up exactly to fit the mold. And remember to use silver solder; ordinary solder has a very low melting point, and may come off when molten lead is poured around it.

Guide Pins. Often molds are made with alignment pins, which stick out of one side of the mold and fit into holes in the other side. Such pins aren't always necessary (except perhaps for some sinker molds), and may do more harm than good. Usually, the round wire and hook, which fit into rounded channels, align the mold perfectly, if things have been precision made. If you're making your own mold, you can probably get by without the pins. If you purchase a mold and find that the pins are in the way, consider removing them.

TROUBLESHOOTING

Anyone who pours spinnerbaits and buzzbaits day in and day out knows that sometimes things simply don't go right. There are days when even the professional luremaker can't get a good head out of the mold and starts to worry about meeting deadlines and paying the rent. Other days, hundreds of perfect heads come off like clockwork. Would a difference in humidity or atmospheric pressure make a difference? The phase of the moon? Probably not. Maybe it's some small thing. You might, for example, use a proven temperature setting on your lead pot, a dependable batch of lead, and a good mold. For some reason, however, you might change the way in which you hold the mold to the lead pot's spout—yes, the angle does make a difference—or you might be a little too quick on the handle operating the flow-control plunger. Sometimes even holding a mold against the pouring spout for too long before you operate the lever makes a difference. What happens, of course, is that the mold acts as a heat sink, cooling the spout to such a point that the lead inside becomes sluggish and doesn't flow out properly.

In short, no one can tell you exactly what's wrong when things aren't going right. There may be a combination of problems, but the nature of the defect generally gives some clue as to what's wrong. The discussion below is classified by the kind of defect or problem.

Flashing. This problem is very common in lead casting. In short, flashing means that lead leaks between the two halves of the mold, causing a thin sheet of lead to stick out on top or bottom. Normally, luremakers scrape this off with a knife blade, but I have seen leadheads from well-known manufacturers, who ought to command better quality control, with flashing so bad it looked like the lure had ill-formed fins. Usually, the company will want such lures cleaned before they are painted and packaged, which means that they have to be scraped by hand or touched to an abrasive wheel, or both. Obviously, flashing costs time and money.

Sometimes flashing occurs because the mold halves don't fit together properly or simply aren't closing tightly. I've even seen cheap commercial molds in tackle shops that had a bow in one or both sides, making a slit wide enough to look through. Sometimes a defective mold can be helped by resurfacing it, but this can be expensive if you get a machine shop to do the work. The complete do-it-yourselfer with a well-equipped shop might resurface a mold with grinding compound and a lapping block, or even with emery cloth stretched over a piece of smooth glass. Obviously, grinding too much of the surface off either side of the mold will change the shape and weight of the leadhead, and grinding off one side without taking an equal amount from the other side will cause a lopsided head.

Of course, flashing will occur whenever the mold doesn't close tightly for any reason, such as using wire and hooks that don't quite fit into the channels in the mold.

Sometimes, a mold will pour without flashing with one alloy but not with another, depending on what's in it. Arsenic, for example, will tend to prevent flashing. Other elements will make the lead flow into the thinnest crack. Also, temperature will have a bearing on whether or not a mold has a flashing problem.

Usually, however, the flashing problem can be solved by cleaning the surfaces of the mold. Little beads of lead are the culprit, and these get on the mold surface when the hot leadhead is removed from the cavity. As far as I know, there's no way to prevent this from happening, and frequent inspection and appropriate cleaning are the only solution. As a rule, such a spot will show up when you look at the mold, perhaps at the right angle, so that only the spots need be scraped off.

Incomplete Heads. Often a spinnerbait or a buzzbait head will be incomplete, usually at the skirt keeper or at the very nose, where the wire comes out of the head. This problem can be caused during start-up by a cold mold or by lead that isn't hot enough, or both.

If a certain bait won't "fill out," it's usually because the alloy, temperature, and flow aren't right. The flow can be influenced by some obstruction, such as a clogged pouring spout on the lead pot. This can usually be cleaned by jiggling a piece of wire of suitable size up into the hole. Be sure to hold the wire at 90 degrees with pliers, lest your hand get burned by a spurt of molten lead. Since buzzbait wire is usually about the right size (0.051 inch), a cleaning tool can be made by cutting off the hook and the arm of a large buzzbait. To use it, hold the tool by the hookless leadhead.

If jiggling doesn't help, try running a steady stream of lead through the hole. After much practice, you can look at a stream and tell whether or not the flow is impaired, and to what degree. Sometimes, you'll have

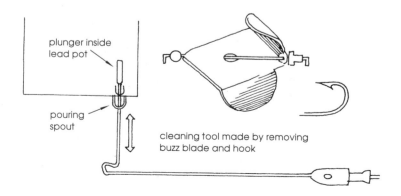

plunger inside lead pot

pouring spout

cleaning tool made by removing buzz blade and hook

to drain the pot and clean the hole and plunger thoroughly. This happens more often when you're using "dirty" lead.

Yes, some lead is much dirtier than others. Scrap lead is often a big problem. Impurities can be partly removed by stirring the melted lead in the pot with a long spoon, which will cause the impurities to break loose and float to the top. A very dirty batch of lead ought to be melted in a larger pot, thoroughly stirred, skimmed, and cast into convenient-size ingots for remelting in your lead pot. Plumbing lead is usually cleaner than scrap lead—but not always.

I've seen various "fluxes" advertised for use in treating lead, but, frankly, I've never seen any that worked for me. The only thing I would advise would be to stir a pot of molten lead from time to time, helping the impurities to break loose and float to the top, where they do no harm.

A clogged pouring spout is such a common problem that the design of the mechanism is of importance to anyone who pours lots of lead. As a rule, it's better not to have curved or doglegged channels leading from the pot to the opening in the pouring spout, simply because they are more difficult to keep clean.

Alloy elements can also cause incomplete heads, especially in the skirt keeper. Too much arsenic, for example, tends to cause the lead to ball up instead of stringing out and running freely into the mold.

Personally, I have never objected to a skirt keeper being a little short, or incomplete, but I know from experience that this can cause problems with heads or lures that are to be resold. Also, a good deal depends on how the head is to be dressed. The way I tie Living Rubber, an incomplete collar won't even show. But some people tie what I call a balloon skirt, and these tend to show more of the collar. The bass probably won't notice, but some fishermen will. Some people are just fussy, and want the bait to look perfect in every way—although it may have an absurd design in wire and blade. I have seen perfect heads on lures that I simply wouldn't throw in the water.

Anyhow, it's best to shoot for perfect lures that are filled out from one end to the other, and sometimes smoking the mold will help. This is accomplished by lighting a large wooden kitchen match and holding it directly under the cavity on one side of the mold. Make sure that smoke covers all parts of the cavity, although you don't want too much of a good thing. Then, without closing the mold, carefully wipe the soot off the surface of the mold around the cavity. The objective here is to remove all the soot from the surface, but none from the cavity. A piece of thin cotton T-shirt stretched over the end of the finger works well for this. After you have smoked one side to perfection, smoke the other side exactly the same way. Once both cavities are smoked, avoid touching the surface. Then pour your baits as usual. If it's done correctly, a smoke job will last a surprisingly long time. I don't recommend smoking, however, if your mold is working nicely without it. As a last resort, the hole into the cavity can be enlarged.

Usually, incomplete heads are defective on the skirt keeper, but the problem can also occur at the nose of the lure. In either place, the larger the wire the more likely a defect. I once knew a mold that used 0.051-inch buzzbait wire, and it always poured in such a way that the head seemed to be smiling. Sometimes the problem can be eliminated by enlarging the mold cavity at the trouble spot. Usually, a skirt keeper can be enlarged somewhat. If it's too big, however, it won't readily accept slip-on skirts, which can be a big problem for high production. Also, if the skirt keeper is too large in diameter, Living Rubber won't tie on exactly the way you want it. When I was in the lure business, our heads were exact in this regard. We wanted the head to be small enough to be used with two half-strips of Living Rubber. For example, if we were tying blue and chartreuse, we would break the ribbon of Living Rubber exactly in half, then cut these halves into the right lengths. Thus, the two halves were put down together, and had to meet up exactly right so that the skirt was even and went all the way around. This was very important to us.

At odd times, a defect will occur just when things seem to be doing very well indeed and conditions seem to be perfect. Sometimes a drop of lead dripping down from the pour spout at the wrong time can cause the problem. If there is a bead on the spout, it's usually best to knock it off with the top edge of your mold as you put the mold to the spout. If the pot drips continuously, it may be possible to install a new plunger. Also, try draining the pot and reseating the plunger with valve grinding compound. You may also be able to rework the plunger mechanism in some way that will permit you to twist the plunger from time to time, thereby helping keep a good seat and seal. I have an old 10-pound pot, modified by David Livingston, that has a screw-in top on the plunger head, which permits me to twist it back and forth with a screwdriver. Another trick I learned from David is to weight the lead pot's lever with a ½-pound piece of lead, which will help keep the valve seated and help prevent leaking when it is in the closed position. This can be accomplished with an elongated piece of lead and two pieces of wire.

Such tricks of the trade are very helpful to anyone who pours lots of lead, and the full-time luremaker should always be on the lookout for such improvements to equipment and technique.

Blow Holes. Sometimes a hole will appear in the surface of a lure, and I think it is caused by air bubbles escaping from the cavity. I once saw a half-ounce spinnerbait mold that consistently poured lures with a blow hole in exactly the same spot, between the gate and the skirt keeper. Sometimes a small hole can be covered up during the cleaning process by scraping over it with a knife under pressure. This pulls some lead over the hole and packs it somewhat, so that it won't show after painting. If the hole doesn't lead to a larger cavity inside, it won't be a serious problem for fishermen. But it can be a problem for the manufacturer trying to sell lures. If you ever have such a problem and consider it to be important, you might try scribing a tiny channel in the mold to make a vent. But don't overdo it unless you want a lead string hanging off your lure head.

Loose Hooks. From time to time you'll find spinnerbaits and buzzbaits with loose hooks. By loose, I mean simply that the hook can be wiggled in the head. Sometimes loose hooks happen more or less at random, but sometimes a whole batch of lures will have loose hooks. The cause of the problem is difficult to pin down, but for some reason an air cavity forms inside the head around the hook eye. My advice is to forget the problem unless you're making lures for sale. I've never known a loose hook to pull out from the head, and the problem is more of an annoyance than anything else. Remember that the head is connected by a "hook keeper" bend or loop in the wire, so that it isn't likely to pull out if you're using 0.035 or 0.040 stainless steel wire.

Orange-Peel Finish. As a rule, the surface of newly poured leadheads will be very smooth, but sometimes there will be wrinkles and folds here and there. On larger lures, such as 3- or 4-ounce jigs, the surface will sometimes be rippled; this is sometimes called the orange-peel effect. It may cause a problem for manufacturers who want one lure to look exactly like its fellows. If you object to the finish, try different pouring temperatures. Also, try smoking the mold.

In my opinion, the orange-peel effect shouldn't be of much concern to the do-it-yourselfer who makes baits for his own use. Just call it a scale finish, paint the head metallic silver—and go fishing.

CENTRIFUGAL CASTING

Many people who start out in the lure business, working in the basement or garage, dream of the day when they can afford centrifugal casting equipment so that they can go big time. It's not my place to shatter someone's dream, but I know people who have gone broke with centrifugal casting equipment. Getting bigger is not always better, and this certainly can be the case with centrifugal equipment. In most casts, a better spinnerbait head can be made consistently with one-cavity aluminum molds.

Nevertheless, many of the mass-produced spinnerbait heads on the market have been made by centrifugal casting, and the process has probably gotten better in recent years. These machines work by placing rather large circular rubber molds onto a spinning platform. Molten lead from a large electric or gas pot is poured into a gate in the center of the circular mold. From there the lead is fed out through a gating system, like spokes in a wheel, to a series of lure cavities near the rim.

The equipment for centrifugal casting is available to everybody who has the money to pay for it, and some of the suppliers are listed in the Appendix. All of the equipment will probably work as billed, but the mold must be made very carefully. There are people who specialize in making such molds; it's also possible to make your own. Before making a decision on all this, it's best to read up on the subject. Books are available, as are videos. Most of these, however, apply to making any sort of small pieces by centrifugal casting and may not even mention spinnerbaits or jigs. These are highly specialized aids produced in limited quantities, and therefore are not cheap.

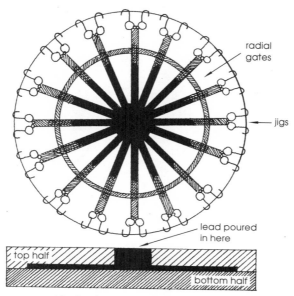

radial
gates

jigs

lead poured
in here

top half

bottom half

side view (area in black shows gates)

Remember that the key to successful centrifugal casting is having a good
mold. And, of course, you'll need a mold for each size and shape of head.
Because you start out with a good mold, however, doesn't mean that it will
last very long. The quality of the molds tends to go to hell with repeated use.
They last longer when they are not overheated, which suggests using small
lures and an alloy with a low melting point.

In fact, the right alloy is essential to success with a good centrifugal
mold. It must be right—and what's right for one head may not be right for
another—in order for the system to work. Since the molten alloy must go
from the center of the mold out to the edge, where it must fill out a shape,
it must not only "pour" well but must remain liquid for quite some time.
In short, know that you might have to stock several alloys if you make several sizes and kinds of heads. There are firms that specialize in alloys, so that
you can get what you need. But you'll have to pay for it, and perhaps for
transportation. Obviously, the centrifugal molds work best for small heads,
where the cost of material per head is not a significant part of total production cost. In other words, a good centrifugal caster might make some money
on today's market with $\frac{1}{32}$-ounce jigs, but not with 6-ounce jigs. Partly
because of material cost, partly because the 6-ounce heads tend to overheat
the mold and distort it, and partly because only a few 6-ounce heads can
be fitted around the rim of the mold. As a rule, the smaller the head, the
more pieces can be produced at one pouring.

Painting
Leadheads

Chapter

10

O nly a few years ago, painting lead was rather difficult, and of course the paint flaked off easily. I've seen packaged jigs that looked good on the shelf, but which were painted with stuff that would flake off with barely a scrape from the fingernail. Back then, most of us who made our own leadheads tried using a base coat of zinc chromate, but it didn't help very much. About the best that we could do was dip the jig into a good hard-finish paint, or perhaps dip it several times, so that a shell would build up around the leadhead. If cracked, this shell would peel off as easily as that of a hard-boiled egg. There were some paints or processes that worked, but they were either expensive, trade secrets, or both.

The first really good leadhead paint I saw was an off-the-shelf poly-urethane paint made by DuPont under the name of Imron. It was recommended to my newly formed lure company by a craftsman who specialized in rebuilding and painting antique cars. David Livingston still uses Imron at Sunkeye, and it is really hard to beat. If it is applied properly, you can knock on it quite a bit before it chips off. In fact, as a sales pitch I would sometimes beat a head against the counter until it flattened slightly—without cracking the paint. I have even flattened the heads with a hammer, but, of course, there is a limit to how much pounding the paint will take.

Imron is not exactly an epoxy but it is mixed in two parts, one of which is called an activator. I understand that it can be used without the activator, but that it would take a week or longer to harden at ambient temperatures. In any case, Imron sprays on quite nicely, although the fumes are dangerous unless a proper mask is used, preferably in a well-ventilated painting booth. One big advantage of Imron is that it works nicely with the wet-on-wet method, as discussed below. It is available in a variety of colors, and in metalflake as well as in a clear coat. Further, one thin coat followed by a clear coat will do nicely. No primer is needed, although DuPont might well recommend that one be used on lead.

Imron can be purchased at outlets that specialize in automobile paint and refinishing supplies. It is expensive. There are several other two-part polyurethane paints on the market, and some of these may work just as well as Imron.

Some vinyl paints also stick nicely to lead, and these, some of which are made especially for fishing lures, are available in strikingly vivid colors. Vinyl can be sprayed, but not as nicely as Imron. Most people dip lures in vinyl paint, which can cause problems with blobs and drip. At least one base coat of white is recommended. After the base coat has hardened, the lure is then coated with colored paint. When the color hardens, it can be followed with a clear coat, which is highly recommended. All of this dipping tends to make a thick coat, compared with Imron, and takes lots of time from start to finish. Also, this paint doesn't "bleed" as nicely as Imron, making it difficult to spray on professional-looking throats and other markings. Wet vinyl paint can be applied over dry paint, so that eyes are no special problem. Vinyl lure paints, and other special lure paints, can be purchased by the gallon for manufacturers or in small jars for the hobbyist. Check the list of suppliers in the Appendix.

WORM WARNING

If you are going to market lures, or plan to make quite a few for yourself, you should know that some types of soft-plastic worms, grubs, and trailers react chemically with some paints. Just because one brand of worm can be used successfully doesn't mean that all of them can. This sort of thing changes from time to time as new products come and go, and it's best to buy a paint made especially for lures and to consult with the manufacturer about using their paint with soft plastics. Improvements continue to be made in this area, and, hopefully, "worm proofing" won't be as much of a problem in the future. Meanwhile, proceed with caution if you mix lead paint and soft plastics, unless you want a mess in your lure package or your tackle box.

SPRAY, BRUSH, OR DIP?

There are several ways to paint lead. Your choice should depend on the kind of paint you're using, how important the paint job is to you, how many pieces you need, and cost. A spray gun and air compressor might be cost effective for a small manufacturer, but not for a hobbyist on a tight budget.

Brushing. If you want just a few lures to fish with, brushing might be the way to go. Of course, a good deal depends on the kind of paint, the brush, and the lure in question, but, generally, you can control the painting process without having drip problems. Also, a brush can be used to dot on eyes, or to paint decorative markings on leadheads that have been painted by other means. In short, any tackle tinkerer ought to have a set of good brushes for painting lures and finishing rod wrappings.

If you do use brushes, remember to get plenty of clean-up solvent that will work on the kind of paint you're using. A good brush will last a long time if it's properly cleaned and stored. One nice thing about a brush is that it permits you to apply paint where you want it, if you're reasonably skilled, without getting it all over the hook, wire, and weedguard.

Dipping. This method is probably used more than any other, especially for jigs. It's easy to stick a leadhead down into a container of paint, but that's not all there is to it. When the leadhead is removed, the paint inevitably will run and drip. For this reason, the lure is usually turned at least once, so that the paint runs first one way and then the other. When the paint runs, it can be thin on one end and thick on the other—thick to the point of forming a visible blob of paint, which is often large enough to disfigure the lure, at least on the surface.

Dipping also gets paint on the wire of spinnerbaits and buzzbaits, and clogs the hook eyelets of jigs. It's best to clean the jig eyelets thoroughly if they're completely clogged with paint. Most manufacturers put painted jigs into a package and leave the cleaning up to the fisherman. This is a pain in the neck, but is probably just as well if the fisherman will make sure that all the paint is out of the eyelet. Jagged edges will cut monofilament line. I once bought a bass bug that had been dipped in paint, and the manufacturer had cleaned the eyelet out with a drill. This left a very sharp surface that cut my leader when I tightened down on the clinch knot. There are other ways to clean out a clogged eyelet, and I usually use split-ring pliers for larger eyes. Tools made especially for cleaning out clogged jig eyelets are available; an awl of suitable size is also good.

Paint can also get into the fiber-guard cluster of weedless jigs, making them far too stiff for hooking fish. Sometimes this paint goes up the monofilament cluster halfway to the hook's point, or even farther.

Of course, the do-it-yourselfer can limit the amount of paint on wire, hooks, and weedguard by holding the leadhead just right and dipping it no deeper into the paint than necessary. This can be done by hand, working one lure at the time, or the lures can be put onto a rack of some sort and dipped all at once.

After the lure has been dipped in paint, eyes can be applied in one way or another. Throats, scale finishes, and other special effects aren't usually found on jigs that have been dipped. It is, however, possible to get a two-toned jig head by dipping the bottom or nose of the jig into another color. I am especially fond of red-and-white jigs finished in this manner; red-and-white lures have been catching fish in fresh and salt water for as long as anyone can remember.

Spraying. If you want a really professional paint job, invest in an airbrush. (High-volume manufacturers might also look into a larger paint gun and

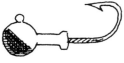

red-and-white jig

large air compressor. This rig can be used for painting the leadheads and an auxiliary air brush can be used for putting on the throats.) Some paints are better for spraying than others, and, as stated earlier, my choice is Imron, partly because no base coat is required if the leadhead is clean.

Very good effects can be achieved on leadheads by spraying wet on wet. The idea is to paint the lure all over with the primary color. Before this coat thoroughly dries, a throat is sprayed on with an air brush. If applied properly, the air-brush paint will be heavy in the center and thinner on the outer edge. The overlayed paint blends in with the first coat, so that there is no seam or ridge where one color bleeds into the other.

An air brush also controls where the paint goes pretty well, so that there is no blatant coat on the hook or wire. The really careful manufacturer, however, will arrange his lures in a rack with shields for the wire for spinnerbaits and buzzbaits—and the fiber guard for weedless jigs. When I was in the lure business, we covered our fiber guards with a soda straw, cut at an angle, before spraying the jigs. Most manufacturers don't take such precautions, especially if they're trying to compete in the mass-market outlets, so that, once again, do-it-yourselfers can make a better lure than they can buy.

plastic tube keeps
paint out of weedguard

If you have the equipment, it's almost always better to spray a lure. But the expense of an air brush must be considered, and remember that you'll also need compressed air. Bottled air will work, up to a point, but if you use an airbrush or larger sprayer very much, you should invest in an air compressor. If you also want one to maintain the air pressure in your auto and truck tires, as well as those on your boat trailer, you'll probably save enough money in the long run to pay for one. At least, that's what I told my wife.

Some people use cans of spray paint for finishing lures, but I don't recommend these. At least I've never found a paint that would stick to lead satisfactorily, although they might look good for a while. A Cherokee Indian who made jewelry and trinkets from beads and spinner blades once showed me some jigs he had painted with spray-can paint. They were so pretty that he planned to corner the market, but he forgot that people usually fish with jigs.

RACKS AND PAINT BOOTHS

If you paint many lures, it will be necessary to build a rack of some sort, or at least rig some way to hang your baits. I've seen several schemes, including making bars of soft plastic and cutting slits for the hooks. One of the easiest ways is to stretch a length of ordinary door spring onto a board. The hooks can be inserted, at an angle, into the slots at an equal distance from each other.

I've seen other rigs as well, including foam cut into strips and bonded onto wood, and little troughs filled with plastic worm material (you can merely melt old worms for this purpose). In any case, if you spray paint, it is best to consider a mounting system on bars. The whole bar can be put into a spray booth and then removed to a suitable drying place. At Sunkeye, David Livingston usually mounts a hundred baits per bar, divided neatly at 25 counts. He has 30 bars, which means that he can paint up to 3,000 heads at a time. Of course, the lures are left in the mount for the first painting, for spraying on the throat, for dotting the eyes, for applying the final clear coat, and for drying. Sounds simple, but painting 30 bars is a day's work. After all, that's 3,000 throats—and 6,000 eyeballs.

EYES, THROATS, AND OTHER MARKINGS

It could be argued that eyes aren't necessary on lures, and one would be hard put to come up with convincing data to the contrary. I personally believe that lures, however outlandish, ought to look like something alive, and that eyes help matters quite a lot simply because most critters do have eyes. Regardless of whether or not bass prefer them, eyes do tend to give the angler more confidence, which is very important in most kinds of fishing. I might add that in my opinion having eyes on either side of a leadhead is more important than having paint on the rest of it. After all, lead isn't a bad color. In other words, to me, plain lead with eyes on either side is better than having a solid head without eyes. Of course, the trend at this writing is for mass-produced spinnerbaits to be packaged without any eyes whatsoever.

Buzzbaits don't need eyes as badly as spinnerbaits, and Living Rubber jigs, designed to scoot along the bottom like a crawfish, don't need eyes as badly as swimming jigs, such as white bucktails that imitate baitfish.

Eyes can be dotted onto the sides of jigs and spinnerbaits with any appropriate paint. A small brush can be used, or a round piece of wood, made from a small dowel pin, can be dipped into the paint and then touched to the leadhead. Nail heads also work, although not as well as wood. Regardless of the dotting implement, it's best to deposit a rather thin layer instead of a drop, which may be hard to contain.

Double eyes can be made by first making a large circle and then following with a smaller circle. Also, it is possible to make thin lids over the eyes, or to make slanted eyes with brushes of various shapes. Once I made some neat slanted eyes by using a nylon brush from the cap off a jar of fingernail polish.

One problem is getting the eyes in the same spot on both sides of the head. Although this might not matter to the bass, most anglers don't like to fish with baits that aren't symmetrical. Believe me. The easiest way is to have some physical variation of the head at spots where the eyes ought to be. This can be done by working on the mold (as discussed in Chapter 9).

The familiar sunken eyes are easy to use in that the depression holds a little paint without allowing it to run. Thus, each eye will be in the same spot and will be the same size.

Bugeyes and frog eyes also work nicely, but they are rounded outward so that the paint is harder to contain. It is, however, possible to put a sunken eye onto a bugeye, as discussed in Chapter 9. The main point to remember here is that such physical markings help the do-it-yourselfer locate the eyes easily.

The neatest rig for dotting eyes I've ever seen was made by David Livingston. He modified the business end of a ballpoint pen, then fitted it into a tube. Thus, he can make eyeballs just as fast as he can dot them, without having to dip a brush or other applicator. He won't tell me exactly how he makes these, but I do know that he uses Imron paint for the eyes. I also know that he dots the eyes while the lures are mounted on a paint bar. The whole bar is put into a vertical position as he dots one side of each head. Then he inverts the bar and dots the other side of each head.

The color of the eyes probably doesn't matter much, so long as it contrasts nicely with the main color of the head. Red is by far the most popular color for eyes. White is good in black or red heads.

In addition to painted eyes, the do-it-yourselfer might consider some of the stick-on materials. Sheets of stick-on eyes for fishing lures are available; the do-it-yourselfers can cut their own with a punch. Sometimes, it's difficult to get these onto rounded heads perfectly, but usually something can be worked out. Many of the lure-component catalogs carry stick-on eyes and materials made for use on fishing lures. The stuff isn't indestructible, but it does stay on remarkably well. This same stuff, I might add, can also be stuck to spinner blades.

In addition to eyes, I always like to have a throat on spinnerbaits, buzzbaits, and jigs. Usually, red works nicely, but I also like orange on brown heads and green on chartreuse heads. Throats can be dipped, but they look like one coat put onto another. The best bet is to spray on the throat with an airbrush. With Imron and possibly other paints, it's best to spray wet on wet. If you're putting a red throat onto a white head, for example, the white is put on first and allowed to set for a while. Before it dries, the red throat is sprayed on, holding the brush so that the heavy concentration goes where the wire meets the head. The red paint will bleed into the white, making a smooth coat that looks and feels like one coat of paint. If the white were allowed to harden, the new coat of red would have a ridge around it, making it look like one coat sprayed onto another. Putting wet on wet, in short, makes the amateur's paint job look like the pro's. Or better. Most of the professional jobs have paint going halfway up the wire arm.

Instead of a throat—or in addition to one—a dark streak on top of the head, visible from either side, is a nice touch. Such a streak, usually black, can be made with an airbrush when the lure is painted. As a rule, it's best to paint the head all over, then apply the streak across the back. Add the throat last. Since many baitfish have dark streaks atop the back, I like to paint tail spinners and lead minnows in this manner. My favorite color for a tail spinner or lead minnow is silver metalflake Imron with a black back and a red throat. My next choice would be gold metalflake Imron with a black back and a red throat.

Scale finishes are made by spraying the lure with the regular color, holding a fine-mesh netting close to the lure body, then spraying another color onto the netting. The netting, usually nylon, can be washed in an appropriate solvent and used again. Other markings, such as herringbone, can be made with the aid of masks or templates. In general, I don't think markings of this sort help spinnerbaits and buzzbaits very much, simply because a leadhead is usually a small part of the overall lure after Living Rubber or other dressing is attached.

CLEANING HEADS

Many of us are somewhat persnickety and want our leadheads to be smooth, and, of course, it is necessary to remove any flashing or parting seams to achieve a top-quality paint job. This can be accomplished easily by first removing the sprue, then running a knife blade over the seams. The spot where the sprue was removed will require special attention, but it really isn't much of a job once you get the hang of it. Of course, much depends on the quality of your mold and the size of the sprue. The better the fit and the smaller the sprue, the less work that has to be done. It's best to work things out so that no actual cutting is required. Light scraping will do.

Remember also that it's best to work the sprue off with a back-and-forth motion instead of a twisting motion; twist-offs are much harder to clean. This won't mean much to the hobbyist but could be important for anyone who has to clean a thousand heads a day.

Some people prefer to use some sort of abrasive wheel for cleaning leadheads, but not me; a good knife does a better job and is just as quick. I might add that some operators take off too much lead with a wheel, disfiguring the head. I've seen small jigs from Taiwan that had only two-thirds of a head left.

Be warned, again, that anyone who cleans leadheads should be very careful to scrub his hands well with soap and warm water before eating or handling food. Also be warned that anyone who wants his paint to stick onto leadheads will wash his hands carefully before cleaning the heads, especially if he has been eating Kentucky Fried Chicken.

Dressing
Leadheads

Although some of the first commercial spinnerbaits and buzzbaits were dressed with bucktail, rubber skirts have been standard on such lures for many years. These skirts were manufactured separately from the rest of the lure and were "slipped on" before the lure was packaged. Indeed, the skirt was often made by a components company and sold in bulk to lure-makers. (It still works that way.) Then came Living Rubber, a product that was originally used in the garment industry for making corsets and other stretch products. Personally, I prefer to tie Living Rubber and other skirt materials directly onto the lure by hand, so that I have full control of what goes on, where it goes, and in what plenty. But a lot can be said for slip-ons, especially from the manufacturer's viewpoint, and good ones are really hard to beat. Besides, slip-ons can be purchased separately and used as replacements for hand-tied skirts. In any case, the breakdown below is set forth in more or less chronological order of appearance.

Hula Skirts. These skirts were used on the old Hawaiian Wiggler in-line baits and are the first ones that I remember using. Similar skirts are made today, featuring thin but rather wide rubber tails, and they are still my favorite slip-on dressing. The first ones tended to have dull colors, but modern pigments and techniques permit even fluorescent chartreuse and fire orange. There are more than a hundred colors and combinations available—solids, two tones, and tricolor.

These skirts are made with thin bands of die-cut rubber. The uncut end is coated with rubber cement and wrapped around a suitable length of surgical tubing. As a rule, two lengths are used on each skirt. Several sizes are made, and these are usually specified by length and number of tails. Most bass anglers use the 3½-inch 40-tail for spinnerbaits and buzzbaits, which is my personal choice in most cases. I do, however, often use a 2½-inch 20-tail skirt on in-line baits and on buzzbaits whenever I want to fish these with a pork frog attachment.

40-tail rubber skirt
with two colors

Usually, these skirts are put on in reverse fashion, which makes them fluff out on the retrieve. When reversed, the length of the skirt shortens up considerably. This is the mode I recommend for most bass fishing; and it's especially effective on a stop-and-go retrieve, when the skirt tends to "breath." However, anglers should also try the skirts the other way so that they stream out behind the lure, looking like an eel or a snake swimming in the water.

As a rule, these skirts are easy to slip on and take off, so that replacing colors isn't much of a problem. I once knew a tournament angler who would fish with nothing else, and he bought them in bags of 100 per color. These skirts have a fairly good shelf life, but after they have been fished with and left in the hot sun, weird chemical things begin to happen.

The current trend in slip-ons is away from these conventional skirts. But don't worry. Just as my old three-button sports coat comes back into vogue every few years—at which time I am definitely avant-garde—the old skirts will be back. Meanwhile, the angler can stock up on some newfangled slip-ons, some of which feature waved or ripple tails that work nicely. There's even a new rubber skirt featuring a pocket for holding a rattle device.

Vinyl Skirts.   At one time, vinyl skirts were quite popular, no doubt because of the vivid colors that were suddenly available. Vinyl skirts are rather hard to find these days, but are still used on some lures, such as the Snagless Sally. These skirts work on leadhead spinnerbaits and buzzbaits, but they are sometimes difficult to put on and take off, owing, in part, to leadhead skirt keepers that are too large. Another problem with vinyl skirts is that the tails tend to stiffen in cold weather, so that the action isn't as good as with rubber.

Breathers.   These are fine-cut rubber skirts, made exactly like the old hula skirts, but with finer, hairlike tails. Breathers became quite popular for a while partly because many manufacturers were trying to compete with the popular hand-tied Living Rubber skirts. But fine rubber strands tended to mat up very badly, making frequent replacements necessary. Some are of good quality, others are not. And it is difficult, when ordering from a catalog, to tell which is which, and I feel that the bad skirts have really hurt the market. Some skirts from the Orient were so bad that they often came apart when you tried to put them onto a spinnerbait. In the water these things were far too bulky, like fishing with a wad of blubber instead of using a skirt with distinct, active tails.

These breather skirts also tend to mat up over the hook and prevent the point from sticking the fish—a consideration that is too often overlooked by anglers using thick skirts. I know one fellow who cuts the top tails off a skirt with scissors to help with this problem.

Of course, the old wide-cut hula skirts and the fine breather skirts have been merged together, resulting in "pro breathers" and others. These are pretty in the water and out, and I like them all right, provided that they are well made and not too much of a good thing. Also, rubber strands are now

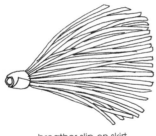

breather slip-on skirt

being used in connection with some new skirt materials, such as Lure-Fil, and this mix is expected to continue for a while. Anglers are always looking for something new for catching fish, and luremakers are always looking for something new for catching anglers.

LIVING RUBBER SKIRTS

Material for making Living Rubber skirts has been around for a long time. Essentially, the material comes in a band, about an inch wide and $\frac{1}{32}$ to $\frac{1}{64}$ inch thick (or thereabouts), that is serrated so that thin strips can be pulled off. The tackle industry has used these strips for a long time for making legs for popping bugs and sponge-rubber spiders.

Living Rubber

The first lure that I saw with Living Rubber strands made into a skirt was sent to me in 1972, when I was working on a book called *Fishing for Bass*. I liked the skirt, but I didn't think too much about it at the time because I figured that it would take too long to bundle up and tie on a skirt and that it had no future in the tackle industry.

What I didn't realize is that a length of the tape can be wrapped onto a lure, stretched out, and cut with scissors, whereupon the seemingly solid tape separates magically into many tails. I don't know who first picked up on this stretch-and-cut routine in a big way, but my first encounter with spinnerbaits and buzzbaits tied in this manner was through a fellow named Hank Trent in California. Hank's baits sported beautiful skirts, with each tail in its place, but they were a little too bushy to suit me. Too much drag. Too bulky. Too much stuff to mat over your hook. Hank used two strips of rubber, usually of different colors, to lend a two-tone effect. I also noticed that Hank sawed a slot into his spinnerbait skirt keepers so that his thread (and therefore the skirt) wouldn't slip back. Shortly after that, I saw some similar skirts at a tackle show in Dallas, put out by an outfit from San Antonio called Good Vibes. They also marketed the rubber in 10-foot rolls, and I started buying it to dress a line of spinnerbait heads that we had developed. In order to hold the Living Rubber skirt in place, we designed a skirt keeper with an indentation up near the head, as shown in the drawing in Chapter 3 on page 19.

The idea is to wrap a strong thread (size D or E) behind the slot, not in it, and then tie in the rubber so that it is forced into the slot; in other words, the rubber is in contact with the leadhead on the bottom. If this skirt keeper is used properly, a person of average strength simply cannot pull the skirt off. I have seen other ways of tying skirts, including binding them down with wire, but the method described here is the most dependable for tying a neat, steadfast skirt.

First, secure the head into a vise—a good one—by the bend of the hook. Next, wrap thread onto the skirt keeper from the collar to the slot.

Then lay down a strip of rubber, as shown (page 106), and wrap the thread over it and slightly forward, so that the pressure forces the rubber down into the slot. The thread is taken around and the rubber follows it. Now give the thread three complete turns under pressure. Next, put down a tie-off thread and wrap it at least five times. (More turns can be made, but it's best to avoid building up too much thread, unless perhaps you want a thread band to be a part of the dressing with spider rubber, as discussed later.) Then, holding the wrapping tight with the thumb and forefinger of your left hand, cut the thread off and run the tag end through the loop. Still holding things tight, pull the tag end under the wrapping. (This is the same procedure used for finishing a rod-guide wrap.) Head cement can be applied to the wrapping, but I never use it because the thread isn't going to slip if it's tied right.

The key is keeping things tight *throughout* the various steps—and *when going from one step to the other.* The pressure from the rubber tends to bind the thread so that it won't loosen. After tying off the rubber, break the strips

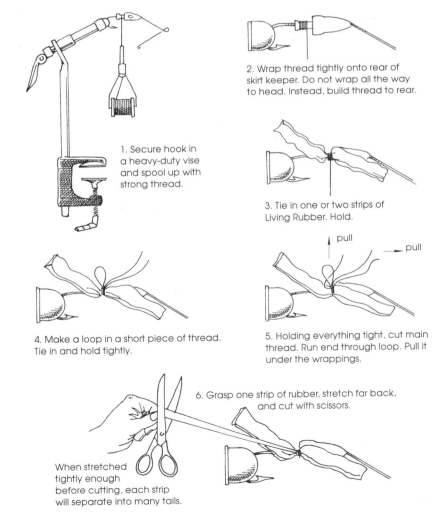

2. Wrap thread tightly onto rear of skirt keeper. Do not wrap all the way to head. Instead, build thread to rear.

1. Secure hook in a heavy-duty vise and spool up with strong thread.

3. Tie in one or two strips of Living Rubber. Hold.

pull

pull

4. Make a loop in a short piece of thread. Tie in and hold tightly.

5. Holding everything tight, cut main thread. Run end through loop. Pull it under the wrappings.

6. Grasp one strip of rubber, stretch far back, and cut with scissors.

When stretched tightly enough before cutting, each strip will separate into many tails.

in half. Pull one back with your finger, hold it tight, and cut it with scissors. If all goes as planned, the strip separates from the end all the way down to the wrapping. Then the other strips are stretched out and cut. If you tie many skirts at one sitting, your fingers will probably get sore on the ends, where your nails dig in to hold the material. Of course, you want to hold the material as close as possible to the end to minimize waste and to have a better gauge on how much to cut off. (If you cut off too much from either strand, the length of the tails won't be uniform.)

After looking high and low for some sort of clamp to hold the rubber strip while stretching it out, I was a little embarrassed when giving a lure-making demonstration in Tallahassee, Florida, when an onlooker, no doubt sensing that my hands were sore, handed me a pair of catfish-skinning pliers off the shelf. They worked perfectly, but, of course, a good pair works better for stretching rubber (and for skinning catfish) than a sorry pair with jaws that don't come together right. I've tried filing the jaws for a smooth fit, but my conclusion is that it's best to throw out a bad pair and buy another one. In addition to making it easier on your fingernails, the pliers will permit you to hold the rubber with only ⅛ inch of the end sticking out. Further, these pliers will grasp a whole 1-inch strip whereas fingernails work only on half a strip. Be warned, however, that stretching that much rubber at one time puts a strain on the hook and will in fact often bend the hook.

I never fish with a Living Rubber spinnerbait or buzzbait without inspecting the hook, and, believe it or not, I've found some hooks, more or less hidden under the skirt, that were bent so badly that the point almost touched the shank. Also be warned that putting such pressure on a bait requires that the hook be clamped tightly into the vise. This in turn wears out vises very quickly. A cheap vise might work for holding dainty flies, but anyone who ties lots of Living Rubber skirts will want a top-quality, heavy-duty vise. I always use a Thompson A with super jaws. I have known people who use a small bench-mounted work vise to hold spinnerbaits, and I've known others who mounted Vise-Grip pliers to a work table. Suit yourself. My advice is to get a really good fly-tying vise that will hold large hooks.

If all goes well, you'll have a perfect skirt that evens out exactly the way you want it. At first, however, things aren't likely to go well, and your skirt will be too long on one end and too short on the other. Remember that the top strip will have to fold over, so that the length of a front strip (which will end up being outside of the skirt) should be a little longer than the rear strip (which will end up being the inside of the skirt). Thus, if the overall strip (before cutting) is 5 inches, you should lay it down with about 2.4 inches toward the hook and 2.6 inches toward the eyelet. This should even out both ends, so that no trimming will be required. It is, however, usually necessary to touch up a skirt, but remember that too much trimming will result in a skirt that is too short. Very often beginners will have to cut off the dressing and try again.

Some people want a skirt with a collar around the front, and this is easy to do simply by keeping the forward end short. The hard thing is to

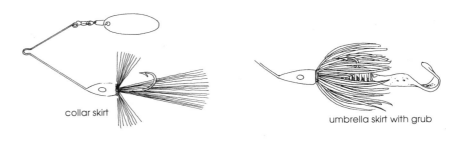

collar skirt

umbrella skirt with grub

make both ends work out exactly the same for lure after lure, if you want them to do so.

In any case, the method above is my favorite for tying skirts. One point that I like is that the bottom layer of rubber pretty much hides the skirt keeper. Some people want to eliminate the bottom rubber, however, and tie all the rubber forward, ending up with what I call the umbrella tie. In this case, the strips are cut to length and put down so that they lay forward toward the eyelet. The ends are wrapped around and covered with thread. Then the tape is stretched and cut. It's a nice skirt if you want to go that way.

Soon after getting into the production of hand-tied spinnerbaits, and after considerable testing on the lake, I knew for sure that skirts made from two strips of rubber were far too bulky and that only one 1-inch strip was necessary. On solid colors, a single strip could be used without waste. But for double colors, two strips, put down one on top of the other, were required. I decided that by splitting a strip exactly in half, I could make double colors without any waste at all. It worked perfectly—except that the strips that I was buying from California were not, at that time, always of uniform width and were therefore not ideal for what I wanted. Sometimes I would have to strip off half an inch or so and throw the rest away, or save it. I must have had a ton of these scrap pieces when I got out of the skirt business.

Anyhow, my standard method of tying two-color skirts is to use two strips, one atop the other. Still another method is to tie on a full piece of a solid color, then tie in a strip of another. This strip is usually put on the bottom (which would be up and accessible when the head is held in the vise). Often you see a blue strip on a chartreuse skirt, and an orange strip on a brown skirt. I like the latter better than half orange and half brown, which is a very popular color because people associate it with crawfish, for some reason.

One of my favorite colors is a solid skirt of regular Living Rubber with a dark streak down either side. Usually, I make the streak with a single strand of spider rubber. White with a black streak is good, or chartreuse with dark blue. The exact colors probably don't make much difference to the bass, but the streak might make the bait more attractive. I might add that some two-tone skirts, tied with half-and-half colors, may not be two-tone

Livingston's streak skirt

at all to some fish. Bass, for example, feed primarily by vibrations, and their eyesight may not be too sharp. In other words, a two-tone bait might well look like a solid shade of gray, especially when the lure is moving through the water. But a solid color with a pronounced streak down either side will, I think, be more visible to bass. Remember that many minnows and bait-fish also have a streak down the side.

In addition to the standard rubber, or regular grade, several new types have come onto the market in recent years and perhaps even more will appear in the future.

Round Rubber. The first round rubber I ever saw came from RJ Tackle in Louisiana. (Originally based in Minnesota under the name of Ric Jig, this firm moved south, then got entirely out of the wholesale and bulk lure-component business.) This new round rubber was very easy to tie, and was a little over an inch wide—ideal for our skirts. I tried round rubber for a while, but discovered that the white tended to yellow with age—and it was available only in black and white. Round rubber and I got off to a bad start. Perhaps I was too early getting into the round-rubber jag, and too quick to get out. The material is now widely available in several good colors, it's easy to tie, and it separates very easily. It's quite different from regular Living Rubber: a skirt of round rubber seems to come through the water easier, the legs don't create as much resistance, and they are a little more springy.

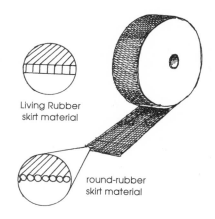

Living Rubber skirt material

round-rubber skirt material

Incidentally, the regular old Living Rubber is now sometimes called "square rubber" to keep it separate in catalog texts from round rubber.

Tarantula Rubber. This kind of Living Rubber, sometimes called "wide-legg," shreds into bands about ⅛ inch wide, similar to the skirt on the old Tarantula spinnerbait put out by Cotton Cordell. Some people like it very much, and I certainly do allow that it will catch lots of bass, especially on spinnerbaits, but I have a problem with it. The wide bands can come down atop the hook's point, preventing a good set.

Spider Rubber. Sometimes called heavy-grade Living Rubber, this is my favorite lure dressing. It catches fish, it seems to last forever, and it doesn't mat up badly. It also has a good action in the water on a stop-and-go or twitch retrieve. It's also very easy to tie and shred. I like to tie in a band of thread, usually of contrasting or complimentary color, which becomes part of the dressing. Also, I like to tie in a tuft of marabou in the center, just for a touch. White spider rubber with a black band and a tuft of red marabou is my favorite dressing for spinnerbaits.

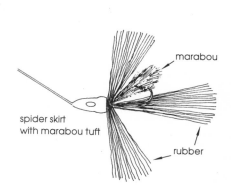

marabou

spider skirt with marabou tuft

rubber

Spider rubber goes nicely in spinnerbaits and larger jigs, but has no real advantage on a buzzbait, which is usually fished with a slow, steady retrieve.

Fine-Grade Living Rubber. This rubber is of a much finer cut than regular rubber, and comes in bands about ½ inch wide. I like it on ⅛-ounce spinnerbaits and buzzbaits, as well as jigs from 1/16 to ⅛ ounce.

Skirts made of this rubber don't last as long as those tied from regular Living Rubber. At this writing, fine-grade rubber is available in 10 colors, but not in the really bright fluorescent or "electric" blue, orange, yellow, and chartreuse that modern anglers seem to expect.

OTHER SKIRT MATERIALS

After hand-tied Living Rubber took hold of the skirt market, and after fine-cut regular slip-on skirts failed in a counterattack, several new materials came along either for hand-tying with thread or for making into a skirt with a banding machine. Some of these new materials are discussed below, and others may be on the market occasionally. The discussion also includes some material that has been used primarily in fly tying and dressing jigs, but which shows up on spinnerbaits and buzzbaits from time to time.

Silicone. This interesting material makes a rather heavy skirt with smooth tails. It is available in 5½-inch strips, and each strip is cut in the middle and solid on the ends. Thus, the strips can be folded and tied directly onto the spinnerbait so that the solid ends are at the head. After both ends are tied down, the material is cut in the middle with scissors. These strips can also be used in a banding machine (discussed later) to make a slip-on skirt. The bands are not wide (about ½ inch), and most people will want to use two strips for each skirt. Precut silicone skirt strips are rather expensive compared with Living Rubber, but the skirt material is available in bulk at considerable savings.

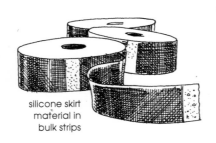

silicone skirt material in bulk strips

In general, silicone makes a good skirt that doesn't stick to everything. Bright color is the main attraction of silicone skirts, plus the fact that glitter can be added to the material, and it shows up very well. Both metalflake and pepper-flake colors are available. The material is also available with fire-tip colors (fire tips and firetails are solid skirts that have a bright color on the very end). These fire-tip strips are doublewidth so that only one strip is needed to make a skirt.

Lumaflex. This threadlike material, made by DuPont, is available on spools. It is usually made into a slip-on skirt with a banding machine. First, however, it is wound onto a piece of cardboard (or some such material) that is 5½ inches long (more or less, depending on how long you want your skirt). The number of wraps determines the number of tails in the skirt. After wrapping, the material is hooked with a hairpin (or some such tool) and slipped off the cardboard. A skirt band is stretched open with a banding machine and the hairpin is inserted and pulled through. The Lumaflex material is more or less centered so that you have two bows. The bows are stretched out tight and cut with scissors.

One big advantage of Lumaflex is that it is practically indestructible and doesn't react with plastic worms or paint. The material seems to glow because of good light reflection, and it absorbs stink-bait scents because the fiber contains air voids. Lumaflex can also be dyed, making firetail skirts easy.

Lumaflex is a trade name taken out by DuPont for its Spandex fiber material, and it's rather expensive. Rat Trap Bait Company (a major supplier of rubber skirts) sells the stuff at $48 per pound, and it costs a good deal more in smaller spools. Rat Trap also markets Lumaflex skirts with or without tinsel.

Lumaflex Skirt

Lure-Fil. This skirting material is available in bulk from Hobbs Feather Co., a firm that supplies many fly-tying and luremaking retailers and wholesalers. If Lure-Fil has characteristics very similar to Lumaflex, it's because it's the same stuff. Hobbs offers Lure-Fil in skeins, and they also have a line of slip-on skirts in many colors, made by banding together Lure-Fil and Fish Flair, a tinsel material. In general, the combinations of colors and materials on the market are getting difficult to catalog. But I'm sure that the black bass will welcome a new pattern called Lisa's Luck, tied with teal blue Lure-Fil and silver marble Fish Flair. If that doesn't whet the appetite, switch to a silicone metalflake pattern, such as Rat Trap's purple with fuchsia.

Dan Gapen once told me, at a tackle show, that modern manufacturers were getting too sophisticated with their colors. "All the colors that you need to catch fish," he said, "are white, black, and yellow." He was right. Although I think it's great if anyone wants to try out every color and material combination under the sun, I think it's a mistake to put so much stock in colors that you become blind to other design considerations. Because a bass pro wins a tournament with chartreuse and lime doesn't mean that he couldn't have won it with black and white.

Tinsels. A few years ago, proponents of tinsel skirts made a play for the spinnerbait market, but they didn't catch on in most areas. Of course, various shiny materials are still used to make skirts, but for the most part such material is now mixed in with more rubberlike material. Although the heading "tinsels" might imply silver or gold colors, some of this material, such as Flashabou, is available in a variety of colors. In addition to being sold in skeins or by the pound, some of this material is available in prebanded slip-on skirts. Hobbs, for example, offers skirts and bulk forms of the following: Fish Flair, a flat metallic tinsel; Monoflash, strands of pearlescent material; Glimmer, some sort of flashy strands available in several colors; Aquahair, strands of flat pearly material in various colors; and Fish Flair/Glimmer, a combination of materials.

A number of other flashy materials, such as Everglow Flash, are available to the fly tyer, and these can be used to some degree in hand-tied skirts. More and more materials of this sort become available each year. If you are interested, get the latest issues of the various fly tyer's supply catalogs and take a look. If you want to add a little flash without having to stock too much stuff, I suggest you buy a little Mylar tape that is silver on one side and gold on the other. Tie it into your ordinary Living Rubber skirts to suit your fancy.

HAND-TIED SLIP-ONS

When I worked some years ago for Lew Childre, the man who revolutionized bass tackle and forced aluminum oxide guides onto the rod-making industry, he wanted to eliminate hand-wrapped rod guides and use slip-on guides, both for inventory control and to reduce labor. But neither anglers nor the fishing-tackle business would accept the slip-on concept. They wanted wrap-on guides. Then Lew came up with an idea for slip-on wrap-on guides, which gave his advertising man an ulcer. I've seen pretty much the same thing happen in the leadhead business, and as soon as it became obvious that the fishing public liked the new hand-tied Living Rubber skirts, luremakers and component dealers have wanted a slip-on hand-tied skirt. It's a matter of inventory. Too many colors.

Anglers simply don't understand the headache that they cause fishing-lure manufacturers and retailers. Consider what can happen to a standard two-color skirt. Some anglers want a white-and-chartreuse skirt; not a chartreuse-and-white; that is, they want the white to be on the outside not on the inside. (Since the skirts are made with tape, one color or the other has to be outside.) Just as soon as the luremaker builds up an inventory of white-and-chartreuse skirts, somebody will discover that chartreuse-and-white is the better color. Then there is the important consideration of head color. Some will want a white-and-chartreuse skirt on a white head. Others will want it on a chartreuse head. A chartreuse-and-white skirt can also go on either a white or a chartreuse head, and from time to time you'll find some oddball who wants it on a red head or a black head. Then we get into the thousands of blade finishes and sizes matched to white and chartreuse. Or chartreuse and white. Tandem or single? Twisted wire or R bend? Light wire or heavy? Size? It's possible to get up a million combinations of a basically white-and-chartreuse spinnerbait. Honest. Add 50 other colors and it would cost the luremaker, the distributor, and the tackle shop a fortune just to stock everything.

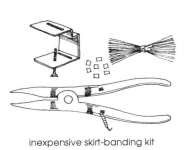

inexpensive skirt-banding kit

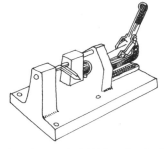

bench-mounted skirt-banding tool

Of course, the do-it-yourselfer can make exactly what he wants without having to stock the rest, and, if he sticks to making lures for his own fishing and is good at it, he can give headaches instead of getting them.

In any case, hand-tied slip-ons were, I suppose, inevitable, and I have come up with a few designs myself, one of which worked fairly well. Also, other tackle tinkerers invented various schemes. A fellow by the name of Danny Gallagher, for example, formed a company to manufacture a slip-on called Tickle Tail. This thing was a combination of Living Rubber, hair, and feathers. It caught fish, sure, but making it was something of a problem and Danny, if I remember correctly, abandoned his plans for setting up a Tickle Tail factory in Central America and settled on a regular Living Rubber skirt for his line of spinnerbaits and buzzbaits. But the Tickle Tail was a great bass catcher, and, again, the do-it-yourselfer can use any combination of Living Rubber, hair, and feathers to make something similar at home.

Of course, the ingenuity of Americans did come through with a way to bind Living Rubber with a small rubber collar. The whole works slips on over the skirt keeper. It's really more difficult to slip the skirt onto the spinnerbait than it is to make it in the first place. In fact, I can hand-tie a skirt directly onto a spinnerbait with thread just as quickly as I can slip on one of the hand-tied slip-on skirts. But they do, I admit, come in handy for replacement skirts.

In any case, the new slip-on skirts are easy to tie with the aid of a banding machine, which, essentially, stretches out a rubber O-ring and holds it open so that the strip of Living Rubber (or strands of the new materials) can be inserted. The procedure is shown in the illustrations. After the skirt material is inserted, the tension on the O-ring is relieved and it closes

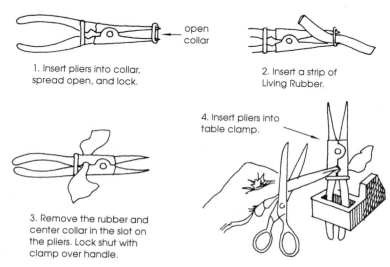

1. Insert pliers into collar, spread open, and lock.

2. Insert a strip of Living Rubber.

3. Remove the rubber and center collar in the slot on the pliers. Lock shut with clamp over handle.

4. Insert pliers into table clamp.

5. Grab rubber with fingers, stretch, and cut with scissors.

down on the material. The Living Rubber is then stretched back and cut as usual.

A very good hand-tied slip-on can be tied directly onto a ³⁄₁₆-inch length of surgical tubing. First, the tubing is slipped on over a tapered peg. The rubber bands are tied on as usual, then pulled out and shredded. Next, the whole unit is slipped off the tapered peg. Then the point of the hook is run through the center of the surgical tubing, which has closed up under the tying pressure. The hook is forced through and the skirt is forced up behind the skirt keeper. Unfortunately, it is very difficult to get it over the skirt keeper, and anyone who wants to go this route is advised to use a head without a skirt keeper. The skirt will usually stay in place on the hook, but it helps to have a bait-holder hook, with a barb or two.

FEATHER DRESSING

Feathers from cocks and other birds can be used on spinnerbaits and buzzbaits as well as on jigs. There is, however, a certain limitation of materials. The do-it-yourselfer who orders from fly-tying catalogs should realize that the high-priced, top-quality neck hackle so prized by fly fishermen aren't worth much to the luremaker, except perhaps as teaser tails to other dressing. Frankly, the large manufacturers haven't done much with feathers on spinnerbaits, but I have used various feathers to advantage and offer the following observations.

some fly patterns can be adapted for small spinnerbaits and buzzbaits

Saddle Hackle. These feathers are often used in making bass bugs and long streamers for bass and saltwater species. They can also be used as tails on spinnerbaits, but they are best when tied in with Living Rubber or some such bushy dressing.

Long saddle-hackle tails can be tied onto the hook before a Living Rubber skirt is tied on—but it simply won't work with a slip-on skirt.

Marabou. These fine, fluffy feathers, which now actually come from turkeys, not the endangered marabou stork, can be used on spinnerbaits and buzzbaits as well as on jigs. Marabou is quite fluffy when dry, but in the water it thins down and resembles a leech or eel. The material is best for fishing with a stop-and-go retrieve, as on jigs, so that it seems to pulsate—and this action can be killed if too much material is used. I've caught bass on spinnerbaits that looked, when dry, like a powder puff from a bordello, but I really don't recommend it for most spinnerbaits and buzzbaits. It is best, I think, when used sparingly. My favorite bait, discussed above, is tied with white spider rubber with just a tuft of red marabou.

Body Feathers. One of the great dressings of all time can be made with speckled body feathers from guinea fowl. For spinnerbaits and buzzbaits, the larger ones from the breast work better, and they are simply tied onto the skirt keeper, trailing back over the hook. The best use of these feathers, I think, is on an in-line spinnerbait, where the blade becomes a part of the dressing. Any sort of body feather can be used, including those from chickens, if they are large enough to dress the bait in question. Just remember that the center rib can be stiff, and that you should not tie anything on in such a way that the dressing prevents the hook's point from sticking the fish.

Wing Quills. These feathers are used for making wings for flies, and for dressing weighted casting flies. When properly selected—usually from duck wings—they can be used as a weedguard as well as for dressing. In my opinion, they have limited use on leadheads—except for weighted casting flies.

HAIR, FUR, AND SYNTHETIC STUFF

Various kinds of animal and synthetic hair can be used on jigs, spinnerbaits, and buzzbaits. I once tied a few Buff Baits with some hair taken from a large dog that was attached to the family. Buff didn't seem to mind, and was probably glad to get rid of some hair in our hot climate, but my wife put a stop to the practice. In any case, you can dress leadheads with most any sort of hair that is long enough, but of course some works better than others. The selection below is not complete, but it includes those materials that are readily available, and it may provide some inspiration.

Bucktail. Hair from a deer's tail has been popular for dressing jigs for a long time. The material has a natural curvature that is difficult to match with synthetic materials, and, of course, the astute do-it-yourselfer will take advantage of this curve instead of squaring off the ends. Natural bucktail tied onto heavy jigs has probably caught more striped bass (and land-locked stripers) than any other type of lure, and "striper jigs" are still sold commercially. Other jigs are also dressed with bucktail, including the famous shad darts.

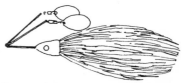

Shannon twin-spin dressed with bucktail

Bucktail is not often used on spinnerbaits and buzzbaits, although it does show up from time to time on such lures as the Uncle Buck's in-line buzzer. And the first offset spinnerbait I ever saw—the old Shannon twin-spin—was dressed with bucktail.

Anyone who hunts deer and also fishes with leadheads will want to try some lures with bucktail. Getting bucktail on the hook is not as easy as you might think, however, and requires some practice. It's best to tie it on in several small batches. Go slowly, noticing that it tends to flare out if you apply much pressure to the thread. You might cut off some small bundles of bucktail and dip the butt ends into a jar of vinyl lure clearcoat (which is, I suspect, the same stuff as vinyl head cement). This will dry into a firm but flexible butt section, which will help hold the bucktail in place. I usually dip a number of these at once, let them drip a little over the container, and dry them on a piece of 2 x 4, arranged so that the butt ends stick out. These can then be stored and used as needed. Since they're long and easy to use, I often tie one or two bundles directly to the hook's shank before I put down a strip of Living Rubber. It's a very good combination on spinnerbaits and buzzbaits.

Bucktails are available from all the fly-tying supply houses, in a variety of natural shades or dyed a number of brilliant colors.

Squirrel Tail.   These tails are covered at some length in Chapter 13. I like them very much for dressing, partly because they're easy to tie and don't flare as badly as bucktail. The hair is a little short for spinnerbaits and buzzbaits, however. Squirrel tails are available from the supply houses, and you can usually get your choice of gray squirrels, fox squirrels, or red squirrels—dyed in a number of colors.

As I write this, I can see a white fox squirrel out my window. That's right. It's solid white, or silvery gray, except for a black mask. My wife says it's the prettiest squirrel she has ever seen and, since I write about cooking game and fish, she made me swear that I wouldn't shoot and eat it. I don't have a recording of the conversation, but I don't think that I took any vows about not shooting it for spinnerbait dressing. There he is. Sitting erect, looking at me from behind his mask. Twitching his tail, then holding it erect, S-shaped.

Other Tails.   Of course, tails of other animals can be used for dressing spinnerbaits and jigs. Check recent copies of the latest fly tyers' supply catalogs to see what's available. Skunk tail is pretty. Fisher tail is more expensive than squirrel, but the hair is a little longer. Kiptail—which is ordinary calf tail—has a slightly crinkled texture, ties easily, and is tough and durable. It is very popular on jigs, but some of it is too short for dressing spinnerbaits and buzzbaits. Kip is available in a number of dyed colors, including fluorescent chartreuse.

Body Hair.   Deer body hair can be spun onto hooks and skirt keepers for jigs, spinnerbaits, and buzzbaits, as discussed under the Rat Buzz in Chapter 13. Deer hair is widely available these days, dyed a number of colors, in bulk, either by the pound or by the square foot, as well as in small packages. Other commonly marketed body hair includes antelope, bear, moose, and elk. But deer hair is hard to beat. Caribou is nice for small bugs, but it is shorter (and more dense) than deer hair and doesn't work well for spinning large bodies.

Zonker Strips.   Strips of rabbit skin, especially tanned to be soft and flexible, are popular on such flies as the Zonker and the Whitlock Water Pup. These strips can be tied onto leadheads and are especially effective when fished with a stop-and-go retrieve, or when twitched along. Anyone wanting a bushy dressing can tie in more than one strip. The strips are expensive, however, and any angler who has a pack of beagle hounds might look into tanning procedures. Whole tanned rabbit skins in a number of colors can also be purchased and cut into strips of suitable length.

FisHair and Synthetic Hair.   These materials, intended to imitate natural bucktail and other popular animal hairs, are available in several lengths and weights. One end is fused for easy use and handling; the other ends are left ragged, making a more or less natural-looking skirt—less natural than bucktail, more natural than nylon. Synthetic hair is available in some very good colors, but some weights are too fine to suit me for large leadheads. For starters, I recommend the 2½-inch, 50 denier FisHair.

This material is really easy to use. Merely snap off what you need and tie it on. It doesn't flare out as badly as bucktail, making it very easy to tie. I like to tie a small bunch onto a spinnerbait hook, then tie on a regular Living Rubber skirt.

FisHair is made by Fish Hair, Inc., and is a trade name. It is available from most of the fly tyers' supply houses. I have seen other similar material for sale, such as Dynel. It may all be the same stuff.

Nylon. Some saltwater lures and jigs are dressed with nylon strands, fused together on the end so that the material is easy to cut and handle. It doesn't flare out much, however, and has a rather square-cut tail end. Because it doesn't have much action in the water, it has limited use for most spinner-baits and buzzbaits. It's best suited for lures fished with a fast retrieve. A number of colors are available.

OTHER DRESSING

When I was in the lure business, we sold quite a few unrigged and undressed heads. One day in November a fellow who worked at a regional medical center came in asking about whether we could provide large numbers of rigged heads without a skirt. I said that we could probably work something out, but that it was best in our opinion to tie on the Living Rubber skirt before the bait is rigged. That way, he would have a standard color that could be fitted with several kinds, colors, and shapes of blades. Otherwise, I pointed out, he would have inventory problems in that he would tie up some expensive blades and expensive swivels.

Inventory was no problem, he said—a statement that perked up my interest considerably. Usually requests of this sort were tempered with the question, "How many do I have to buy?"

"Who's going to dress the baits?" I asked, half afraid of getting more business and half afraid of not getting it.

"We're going to train people to do it. Handicapped labor, maybe."

"Where are you going to get your rubber?" I asked, hoping that we could supply him.

"We're not going to use rubber," he said, uneasily.

An awkward silence followed, but he offered no explanation of what they were going to use for dressing. I didn't push the point, but I told him that inventory *was* a problem with me and that I would require half pay-ment in advance before I could rig large numbers of baits with swivels and blades, and that we would require 90 days on large repeat orders. "I'll need the first order right away, too," I said, "so that I can order swivels. If you want ball bearings, I ought to tell you that I've sometimes waited months for them to come in. Now is the time to order. If you wait until January or February, forget it—unless you want baits in July."

The fellow didn't like what he was hearing and he said that perhaps they would have to go back to the spreadsheet. Apparently they were planning on having a hot lure and would need quicker delivery.

I pointed out that buzzbaits didn't require a ball-bearing swivel and would be cheaper to rig and inventory. The best bet would be to start with buzzbaits for next season—and the season for buzzbaits is usually summer—and then add the spinnerbaits later, after they gained some experience in the lure trade.

"Well," he said, "we're coming out with something new. . . . "

I got it. He was afraid that somebody would steal the idea if they made a test run with buzzbaits. I had heard all this before and I probably smiled.

"We may do our own rigging and dressing, as you call it," he said, "but we do want your heads. What is your capacity?"

"Our *what*?" I had heard him correctly but I didn't know quite what to say.

"How many heads can you make per year?" he asked.

"I'm not selling you people our entire production," I said. "I can't cut off my regular customers. Especially since I've seen 'something new' come and go each year since I've been in business. I've seen it all."

He looked around to see whether or not anyone was watching. Then he pulled a spinnerbait out of his shirt pocket, put it on the table, and said, "You haven't seen these!" It featured a pale yellow Velcro skirt tied onto a spinnerbait head that we had made. "The advantage is that the skirt gets entangled in a bass's teeth and he can't spit it out."

"I hate to tell you," I said, "but . . . wait a minute." I went over to a table where I had a briefcase full of newfangled stuff I'd brought in from the big tackle show held each August by the American Fishing Tackle Manufacturer's Association. After shuffling stuff around, I found a spinnerbait with a Velcro skirt. If memory serves me accurately, it was made by Cotton Cordell.

"Where did you get that!" he said.

"From the AFTMA show. That's the large annual show for fishing-tackle dealers and distributors."

"Can I have this?" he asked, grabbing the lure.

"Sure," I said as he went out the door. That's the last I saw of the Velcro skirt, although they may be still on the market. That's also the last I saw of the paramedic, but I heard later that someone had talked a prominent local surgeon into financing a Velcro spinnerbait venture. As far as I know, however, the good doctor didn't put any of his money on Velcro. If he did, they put the stuff on somebody else's heads.

To be sure, fish will hit lures dressed with Velcro, but, personally, I feel that the wide strips tend to stick onto the point of the hook, thereby preventing the fish from being stuck. In short, I feel that any possible advantage of Velcro (as a skirt material) is offset by disadvantages. It may have an application, however, when fishing for gar. The idea here is to tie a strip of

Velcro to a leader on a fly line without a hook. The gar always grabs such a strip sideways and clamps down. That's when its teeth get entangled in the material. (Other woven materials and ropes can also be used.) Note that a hook is not required. If you're after gar, you might even try a strip of Velcro on a spinnerbait or buzzbait. The idea is to tie a long shiner- or shad-shaped skirt onto any bait that can be fished very slowly.

Other materials can also be used to dress spinnerbaits, and the creative do-it-yourselfer can come up with some good ones. Rubber bands, for example, can be bunched and tied into a dandy skirt. Thin strips of leather have also been used to make skirts, and, when soaked in water, these work very well. Attempts to market leather skirts, however, have not been successful.

SOFT-PLASTIC AND PORK-RIND ATTACHMENTS

Although attachments are not necessary for any well-dressed lure to catch fish, they often add a little something extra and give the angler a quick way to change the overall color and shape of the offering. The various soft-plastic curl-tails, split-tails, worms, lizards, and others can merely be threaded onto the main hook, or, perhaps, onto a trailer hook. Some of the split-tails are very popular as trailers, and so are the curl-tails. These days, many plastic worms have curly tails, which often can be salvaged and used as trailers when the hook end of the worm begins to tear. Twin curly tails make a great bait, and I like them teamed with a sparse skirt in shallow water.

Most anglers ought to know that in addition to being used as an attachment under a regular skirt or other dressing, soft plastics can be used without any additional dressing. As a rule, these have very little drag and work

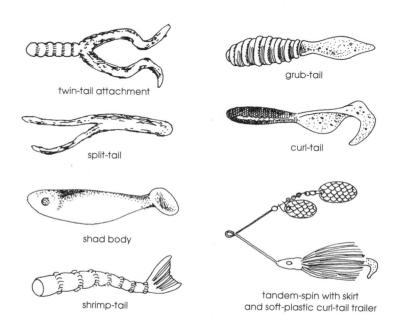

twin-tail attachment

grub-tail

split-tail

curl-tail

shad body

shrimp-tail

tandem-spin with skirt
and soft-plastic curl-tail trailer

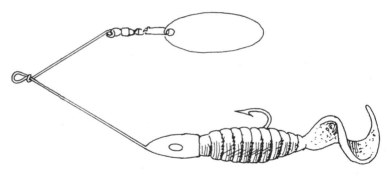

a single-spin dressed with a grub and small blade is good
for fishing rivers and deep water

better in rather deep water with small blades. They don't cast as gently as a
lure with a skirt, which is a count against them for shallow water, except
perhaps for long fan casts on the flats.

Moreover, there is a move in the industry to use molded plastic "skirts"
of one form or another. Doc Morehead started this in Kentucky about 18
years ago, by putting several curl-tails together, radially, so that the tails
stuck out like a skirt. They were beautiful baits in the water, but they
created lots of drag and tore up easily. Gapen's Tackle later bought
out the Morehead line. Since then, other soft-plastic skirts have come
along, such as the spider shown at left.

In addition to soft plastic, pork rind can be used to great advantage
on spinnerbaits and buzzbaits as well as on jigs. I like pork frogs (or
chunks) on sparsely dressed in-line baits and thin strips on deeper-run-
ning lures. The long ripple rind is wonderful for throw-and-crank lures.
I have also fished 9-inch black pork eels on the bottom with a single-spin,
twitching it along like a worm. These can be deadly on very large bass.

Pork attachments have a hole or slit in the big end so that they
can be inserted over the barb of the hook. As every angler knows, they

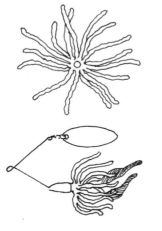

single-spin dressed with soft-plastic
spider and twin curl-tails

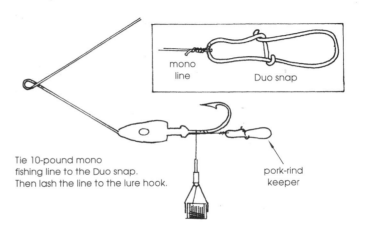

mono
line

Duo snap

Tie 10-pound mono
fishing line to the Duo snap.
Then lash the line to the lure hook.

pork-rind
keeper

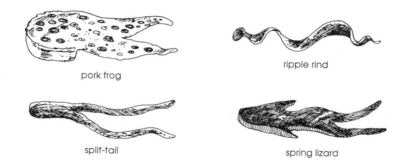

pork frog

ripple rind

split-tail

spring lizard

go on easier than they come off, especially with larger hooks. I like to tie a Duo snap onto the shank of my hook, as shown in the drawing. In addition to acting as a quick change device, the snap also puts the pork attachment back where it ought to be. Without such a snap, the pork strip rides in the bend of the hook, out of line with the rest of the bait. The snap, or some other such device, works with hand-tied skirts, but not with slip-ons.

People who put a lot of stock in scent baits might want to consider strips of fish cut from the sides or belly of baitfish. A belly strip from a large wild shiner, for example, works quite nicely on a spinnerbait, buzzbait, or jig.

FUNCTIONAL DRESSING

The skirt and other dressing is usually considered to be mere show, but it does, or can, have other functions that the complete do-it-yourselfer will want to consider.

Air Resistance. The next time you're in a quiet slough, tie on a ½-ounce PT spoon (or some such spoon dressed with a slip-on skirt) and remove the skirt. Cast it to a likely spot; notice that it shoots in like a bullet. Now slip on a skirt and make the same cast. The bait will slow noticeably—giving you more control of the cast if you are using a revolving spool reel and know how to use it—and sit down gently on the water. This gentle presentation is at its best when you make a tip-roll cast with a bait-casting rig so that the lure is released near the surface of the water, rises up, expends its energy, and, with thumb control, sits down gently into the pocket. Hold on.

Of course, in some other applications the angler may not want much air resistance, as when making very long casts to schooling fish. In this case, dressing the lure with soft plastic instead of with feathers or hair or rubber would be in order. A plastic shad on a ¾-ounce jig can be cast half a mile with a good spinning rig properly spooled with light line.

Water Drag. In addition to providing air resistance during the cast, the skirt also provides water drag while the lure is in the water. This can be very important in some kinds of fishing with jigs, in that it helps slow down the lure on the fall. At other times, the angler may want a sparse dressing so that the bait will fall quicker and speed things up. It depends on the conditions.

Smell. I'm not much of a stink-bait fisherman. Even for catfish, I prefer a live crawfish to a wad of foul-smelling dough or a strip of rancid liver. But there may be good reason to fish with salt-impregnated worms and various flavors of this or that. In any case, the modern stink-baiter has available a wide variety of sprays and dips, often made with natural ingredients. The complete do-it-yourselfer can toss a few shiners (or some other bait) into a blender with a little water or oil and zap them until he has what he wants. This stuff can be poured onto lures, brushed on, or otherwise administered. One of the best bets, I think, is to dress spinnerbaits, buzzbaits, and jigs with deer body hair or other hair dressing and soak them overnight in the scent. Of course, if you're fishing a jig on the bottom, you'll want to scent it with crawfish juice. If you're after bass in open water, try a shad-colored bucktail doused with shad juice. Or shiner juice. Or spit on it.

Some of the synthetic skirt materials will hold scent much better than others, and claims have been made for Lumaflex material's ability to hold scent.

Also remember that some fish have an incredible sense of smell, so that a little stink goes a long way. The natural smell of hair and feathers will be an attraction, and merely putting these materials in water will activate the smell.

Working with Wire

Preformed spinnerbait and buzzbait wires normally stocked by suppliers aren't always cut and bent in the right proportions, at least not for me. Some "standard" buzzbait wires, for example, put the blade too close to the hook, either because the distance between the head and the line tie is too short, or because the top-riding blade arm is too long, or both.

If you have a choice in spinnerbait wire but don't know exactly what you want, it may be a good idea to buy wires longer than you need and cut them down to size. The same wire can be used for long-armed tandem-spins or it can be cut back for use in short-armed single-spins. The diameter of these wires is pretty standard these days; most spinnerbaits are either 0.035 or 0.040; buzzbaits are usually 0.051 for ¼-, ⅜-, and ½-ounce sizes, and 0.040 for ⅛-ounce sizes.

Diameters and lengths of the various wires are discussed in previous chapters; this chapter is concerned mainly with bending such wires of standard diameters. Of course, it stands to reason that open-bend wires for spinnerbaits or buzzbaits must be strong enough to hold their shape under the pressure of fighting a fish or pulling on a stump.

Tools and equipment for working with wire can be cheap or expensive, and judicious selection should depend partly on your pocketbook and partly on what you want to bend, how you want it, and how many pieces you need. As a rule, making twisted spinnerbait eyes, where the wire is wrapped around itself, is more difficult than making R bends or U bends. For that reason, I suggest that do-it-yourselfers start off with these simpler bends. If you really need or want a large number of nonstandard pieces with twisted eyes, it might be better to have the wire custom bent for you by one of the firms listed in the Appendix.

MAKING OPEN BENDS

Lay one end of a straight length of coathanger wire down on a piece of scrap wood and drive two nails snugly on either side of it. Now rotate the other end of the wire 180 degrees on the surface of the wood, and you have formed a hook or U bend in the wire. It may spring back a little, depending on the size and temper of the wire, but you can adjust this by trial and error. This basic U bend can be used in combination with other U bends for making wires for spinnerbaits and buzzbaits.

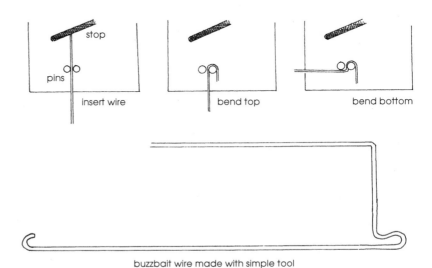

buzzbait wire made with simple tool

Of course, nails driven into a piece of wood aren't sufficiently precise for smaller wire, but the same principle can be used by drilling holes into a piece of metal and inserting posts instead of driving in nails. A precision drill press with a chuck is desirable for this, but you can use a hand-held drill. Instead of nails, try using hard metal pins; I often use the solid end of worn-out drill bits. The diameter of the post determines the radius of the bend, giving the do-it-yourselfer some control over this. (I always like tight bends— but be warned that making them too tight might cause the wire to break during normal fishing. See Chapter 2 for a full explanation.) The distance between the posts can also be important; there must be enough room to permit the wire to be inserted and removed. For bending loops for attaching a swivel in the end of spinnerbait wire, the fit should be pretty tight lest it slip out when the bend is formed.

The illustration shows a simple wire-bending jig. With this one the jig is held stationary and the wire is rotated. The same bend can be achieved by holding the wire stationary and rotating the tool. As stated in Chapter 5, David Livingston at Sunkeye Heads makes a tool designed especially for forming the loop on the end of a spinnerbait. The tool is held in the hand, the end of the wire is inserted, and the tool is rotated. He markets these for both 0.035- and 0.040-thousand wire. Of course, the complete do-it-your-selfer can come up with a similar device for home use. And the roundnose pliers available from the lure-component supply houses, can also be used to make neat loops.

In a little more elaborate setup, the bending machine is mounted on a bench and the "looper"—equipped with a handle on one end and prongs on the other—is free to rotate in a hole of suitable size. This rig is fitted with an adjustable stop, so that leg lengths can be adjusted and duplicated. Bench-mounted machines for making these kinds of bends are available, or anyone with metal-working capabilities can make one. The outside prong on such a machine is prone to wear. Assuming that the center prong stays more or less centered during a bending operation, the outside prong has to force the wire around. As the wire bends, it drags on and wears the surface of the prong. Before going to lots of trouble designing and building a bending machine for high-volume use, take this wear factor into account and figure some means of replacing the prongs, or at least the outside prong. High-quality metal will extend tool life. Also, the outside prong can have a larger diameter, since the radius of the bend is determined by the inside pin.

insert wire   rotate tool   ← stop pin set for R bend

In any case, a machine of this sort can be adjusted to make all manner of open bends for spinnerbaits and buzzbaits. It can also make R bends in only one operation if a stop post is installed in the right place.

In addition to bench-mounted tools, inexpensive hand-held models are available that will make open bends as well as loops or twisted eyelets.

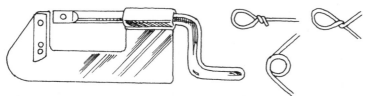

hand tool for bending and twisting wire; twisted eyes and closed loops

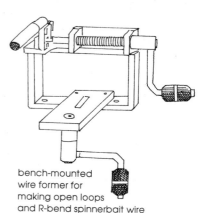

bench-mounted wire former for making open loops and R-bend spinnerbait wire

MAKING CLOSED BENDS AND LOOPS

Coil Eyes.   The easiest of the closed bends is a simple coil, which can be made with some of the bending machines discussed above; the wire is wrapped around like a short spring. I like this design with spinnerbait wire because it gives one a good feeling for the blade; it's not very common on spinnerbaits, however, except for what I call the H&H-type lures. The coil bend is also commonly used on jig spinners. One disadvantage is that the line tie is made up of two thicknesses of wire, which is not a bad idea, it seems to me, with wire in the smaller diameters.

Twisted Eyes.   Do-it-yourselfers can make twisted eyes for both spinner-baits and in-line baits, but it's more complicated than making open-bend eyes. Both hand-held and bench-mounted machines are available for the hobbyist and small manufacturer, and Worth markets a heavy-duty rig for manufacturers. I'm not going to try to describe the workings of these machines, but the principle can be illustrated by holding a hairpin tightly in a large pair of pliers so that a loop sticks out. Insert a nail into the loop, twist the nail, and you'll start forming a twisted eye. Or, if you prefer, put the end of the loop over a fixed shaft and rotate the pliers. The machines are a little more complicated, of course, and you usually start by forming an open loop with a leg.

As stated earlier, it's much easier for hobbyists to purchase spinnerbait wire with the twisted eye already formed. Wires for in-line baits can be purchased with a preformed loop on one end. But what about the other end? It's easy to make a similar loop at home with one of the bench-mounted machines.

Whether you twist your own loops for in-line baits or buy preformed wire, you'll notice that a sharp end of wire sticks up. I've never liked this because the end can nick or cut your line, and I usually file it off or mash it down with pliers. Purists will mash it down, then file it off and fill it in with solder.

KINDS OF WIRE

Most of the preformed spinnerbait wire I've purchased has been neatly pack-aged by the hundreds. Some of the straight wires are packaged loose by the thousand, but these are easy to untangle. This untangling business can get serious if you've got a thousand pieces of anything with partly closed loops in it. Once I bought a thousand spinnerbait heads poured on wire with a pre-formed loop in the end, which (I reasoned) would save time in rigging single-spins—and it took two days to untangle them.

In any case, the luremaker can purchase wire in various forms and in all manner of weights. The sketches at right show some of the forms that are readily available, either in bulk by the thousands or by the hundred count.

The first requirement is that the wire be heavy enough to do the job. Remember, however, that the heavier the wire the harder it is to form.

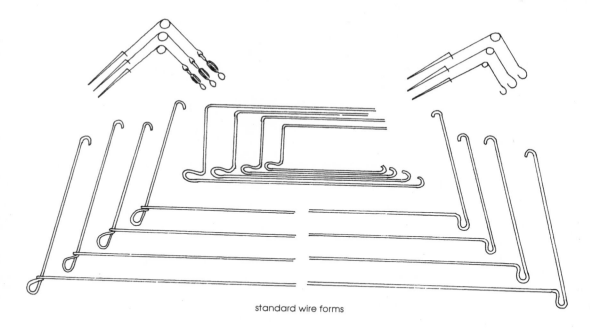

standard wire forms

Remember also that a limber wire can add to the action of the lure. In either case, I recommend that you use only stainless steel wire. It's always best to buy wire in straight lengths instead of in coils or on spools, unless you've got a machine to stretch and straighten it.

CUTTING WIRE

Surprisingly, many so-called wire cutters don't really cut wire; instead they pinch it in two. True wire cutters don't pinch, they shear. The difference is that pinchers leave a pointed end that can cut your fishing line, and the shears leave a square end. Square-cut wire also has sharp edges around the circumference of the cut; in either case, it's a good idea to look at your lures for surfaces that can cut your line. Sometimes a file will help, and, as stated elsewhere, sometimes a little solder will smooth things up.

Other Leadheads and Deadly Rigs

Chapter

13

A few years ago, a local character called Otter Hanes approached me with a brown paper bag, twisted at the top. In it, he said, was a million dollars. Then he dumped a dozen lures onto my desktop. All of them were dressed somewhat crudely with squirrel tail, and all of them were, I noticed, tied onto buzzbait and spinnerbait heads that my firm had made. The guy had torn my beautiful hand-tied Living Rubber skirts off and wrapped squirrel tail onto the hook.

"These things will sell themselves, Livingston," he said. "All you've got to do is make them. I'll provide the squirrel tails. We'll go fifty-fifty."

I declined the offer—but I didn't doubt for a minute that the lure would catch bass. In fact, I once saw a largemouth, taken from Pea River, that had eaten a small squirrel. Although I never tried to market such a lure, I did make a few squirrel spins for my own tackle box, and I was pleased with the results, for several reasons. First, the hair was easy to tie, and didn't flare up as badly as bucktail. Second, I liked the natural color of the gray squirrel tails (with white tips) and the larger fox squirrel tails. Third, the dressing was more durable than rubber, feathers, or even bucktail. Fourth, the lures didn't have too much air resistance on the cast, or too much water drag on the retrieve, as do similar lures dressed with Living Rubber. Fifth, squirrel tail caught fish—especially bass.

Trying your own squirrel-tail lures requires little investment in time or money. You can use old spinnerbaits or buzzbaits, or remove the skirt from new baits. Squirrel tails are widely available from stores and mail-order houses that carry fly-tying supplies, or you can bag your own in season. If you get your own squirrel, cut the tail off and cover the stub end heavily with salt. It's not necessary to skin or bone the tail, but I do hang mine out in the sun for a couple of weeks, adding more salt to the butt end from time to time. After the tail has thoroughly dried, store it in a plastic Ziploc bag or a tight box to keep the bugs out.

While my would-be business partner merely wrapped a swatch of squirrel tail around the lead skirt keeper on the spinnerbait, I prefer to wrap some tail onto the hook's shank first. Then I wrap a shorter bunch onto the skirt keeper. This gives a more pleasing pattern of hair, alternating white tips with gray. It also allows me to make the skirt a little longer on my ⅜- and ½- ounce baits.

Start by putting the spinnerbait's hook into a vise. Tightly wrap some thread onto the hook behind the lead skirt keeper. Apply a little head cement. Tie in some hair, making the butt ends flush with the spinnerbait's skirt keeper. Tie off the thread and coat with head cement.

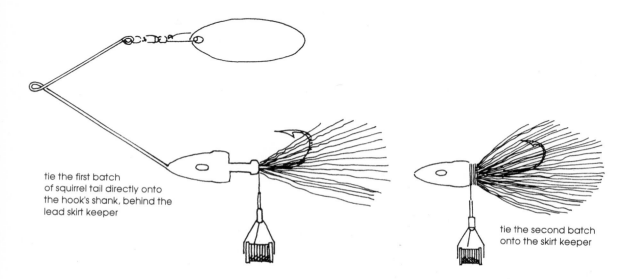

tie the first batch of squirrel tail directly onto the hook's shank, behind the lead skirt keeper

tie the second batch onto the skirt keeper

Next, wrap thread around the skirt keeper. Select a swatch of hair similar to that tied onto the bare hook. Trim the butt ends. Tie this hair onto the skirt keeper, making sure that equal amounts go all around it. (Some people may find it easier to tie in the hair in top and bottom segments.) Wrap the ends with thread and tie off near the body of the spinnerbait's head. Coat the wrapping with head cement.

The technique above can be used on single-spins, tandem-spins, and buzzbaits, or jigs. My favorite squirrel-tail lure is a single-spin with a smaller than usual blade, fished a little faster than regular spinnerbaits. But I must add that I probably have a tendency to retrieve a lure too fast—like a squirrel trying to get out of Pea River.

TAIL-SPINS

Tom Mann is a smart fellow. Being a bass pro in the fishing-lure business, he sold the public on the idea of jelly-soft plastic worms as well as on the Little George tail-spin lure. The tail-spin, of course, isn't much more than a hunk of lead with a treble hook dangling down from the belly and a spinner blade on the end. It would be hard to design a lure better suited to hang up on limbs—and Mann had the gall to tell people that they must fish the lure deep; if they weren't scratching brush, they weren't fishing deep enough. When somebody asked him about losing so many lures, Mann grinned a little sheepishly and said that, shoot, he could fish all day on two cards.

Actually, the Little George wasn't an entirely new idea. The first tail spinner that I ever saw was the Spin-Rite, made by a Kentucky lure company, and now marketed by Uncle Josh. In any case, the do-it-yourselfer who wants to scratch bottom with a tail-spin lure has a great advantage because he can make all he needs easily, and at a fraction of the cost of a retail bait. Molds for these lures are available in several sizes. Preformed T-shaped wires are also available, although in some cases the wires don't fit just right in the molds, or at least not quite like I want them. It's not difficult to bend the wire, but of course a jig is required for production work.

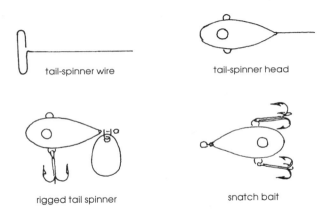

tail-spinner wire

tail-spinner head

rigged tail spinner

snatch bait

The shape of these lures varies from one brand to another, and I doubt that it makes too much difference. The important thing is that the wire be the right shape and size to accommodate the hook and tail-spinner blade, and to keep them from getting in each other's way.

One problem with tail-spins is that they are fairly easy for a black bass to "throw"; that is, the bass jumps up and shakes its head and slings the lure back at you. This problem can be eliminated by rigging a slip shad, in which the line going to the hook runs free through a hole in the lure's body. The lure is molded with the aid of a pull pin to form the hole, much like the ones used to make slip sinkers. I don't know who came up with the idea of the slip shad, but the first one I ever saw was made by Four Rivers tackle in Mississippi. The first slip lure I ever saw, however, was a "jig" for stripers made by a retired math professor who lived on Mobile Bay.

When rigged a little differently, these baits make an ideal "lure" for snatching fish, but be warned that this practice may be illegal in many areas (and probably should be in all of them). As shown in the drawing at left,

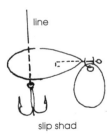

line

slip shad

the idea is to make a twisted line-tie eye on the end of the lure instead of on top and put treble hooks on the other end.

LEAD MINNOWS

These baits are made very much like tail-spins, except that they have a treble hook where the blade ought to be. Mann's put out a bait like this, and so have other lure companies. Gapen's Tackle, for example, came up with several types of small lures that are more or less minnow shaped. These are great for crappie and white bass. They are especially effective on schooling fish because they can be cast half a mile with balanced spinning tackle.

Many years ago, I fished with my father and Judge Mitchell for saltwater seatrout (speckled trout) in the north of Florida, and we trolled with a lead bait about 3 inches long. It was dip-painted with a red head and a white body. Such a lure, with the same paint job, will still work today.

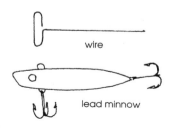

wire

lead minnow

LEAD SPOONS

Lead jigging spoons are easy to make, and molds are available in several sizes. There are a number of color schemes for spoons, but I think silver or gold metalflake works best. If painted with a thin coat of flexible Imron, these lures can be bent slightly to give more action in the water.

These spoons can be cast, or trolled, but they're primarily jigging spoons for vertical fishing. These should flutter down, and the fish, especially bass, hit them on the fall. In large impoundments with standing timber, the trick is to free-spool these down beside a tree trunk, working them all the way to the bottom, then raising them about 3 feet and letting them drop. If your line twitches, you are "getting a bite." If you don't react immediately, the bass will surely spit the lead out.

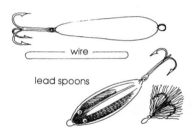

wire

lead spoons

Lead spoons are also used for making long casts into turbine boils below large hydroelectric dams. Often a 3- or 4-ounce spoon (or a jig of similar weight) will be used with saltwater spinning tackle or surf rods, in order to sling the bait far enough to reach the boils. Since many of these dams are built on large rivers that form state lines, it's possible to stand in one state and fish in another.

STUMP-JUMPERS OR HORSEHEADS

These baits are popular in some areas, especially in the smaller sizes. Inexpensive molds are available that have slots for a jig hook, and another for a crane or barrel swivel, to which a blade will be attached.

horsehead with blade and curl-tail grub

These baits can be dressed with bucktail, feathers, Living Rubber, or soft plastic. Indiana blades seem to be the accepted shape, but other blades can be used. Just make sure that the blade revolves on the retrieve instead of fouling on the hook or dressing.

SONIC VIBRATORS

brass insert

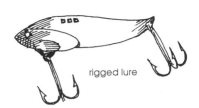

rigged lure

These excellent lures combine a leadhead and a metal plate arranged to produce a tight wiggle on the retrieve. They are easy to make, and both molds and brass plates are readily available. Several line-tie holes along the top of the bait determine the angle at which the bait tracks and, consequently, the tightness of the wiggle. The center hole usually works best, but suit yourself. The main point to remember is to use a snap. Tying the line directly to the bait tends to dampen the action.

Remember that one snap is not as good as another, and that there is a lot of junk on the market. Some snaps are of faulty design, and some are made from soft metal. I prefer the "Duo" snaps from Rosco, which are made of stainless steel wire and are rated by pound-test. The 20-pound test is just right for me, although some may want the 25-pound test.

MAKING THE RAT BUZZ

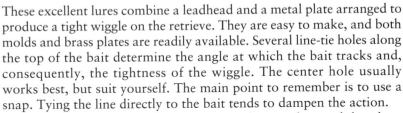

Largemouth bass, muskie, and other aggressive fish love mice, small muskrats, and, as mentioned above, even baby squirrels or marsh rabbits that fall into the water. A neat ratlike bait can be made by tying ordinary deer body hair onto a buzzbait. Spinning the deer hair (as shown in the drawings at right) makes it flare out, and the addition of a suitable tail completes a lifelike bait. The buzz rat looks even better when retrieved in the water, where the large delta blade causes a commotion not unlike something with legs scrambling for cover or dry land. This can be a great bait, especially around shallow, weedy spots, or under thick brushy banks. Try it early in the morning or late in the afternoon. In hot weather, fish it at night.

Making the head and rigging the blade on the wire is easy for hobbyists who mold their own spinnerbaits and buzzbaits. Others can start with an old buzzbait. (Most of us can usually find several buzzers in our tackle boxes that need new skirts or other dressing.) A heavy-duty fly-tyer's vise that will hold a large hook will be helpful, but a small bench vise will work. Although a thread bobbin is helpful, you can work directly from the spool of thread. Strong thread is essential for spinning deer hair, and I recommend a size D nylon rod-wrapping thread. (In a pinch, try dental floss.) Color isn't important, but I normally use black.

Before putting the buzzbait into the vise, trim away the part of the lead that holds the skirt in place. Then secure the bait in a vise, gripping it in the bend of the hook. Next, tie in a thin strip of black or brown leather for the tail. I have used strips of Living Rubber, vinyl, and other material, but most leather is tougher, has a nice wiggle when it's wet, and lasts longer. After

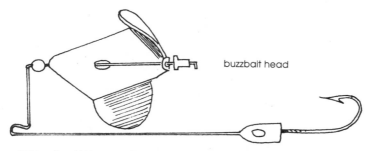

buzzbait head

remove the skirt keeper with a knife, or make a head without a skirt keeper

you get the tail in place, wrap the thread forward. Pinch up some hair on a deer hide, cut it out with scissors, and comb out the short fuzz at the base of the hair with your fingers. Holding the hair tightly over the hook with the thumb and forefinger of one hand, wrap thread around the bundle for a couple of turns. Then apply pressure to the thread while slowly releasing your finger grip, causing the hair to spin around the hook's shank and flare

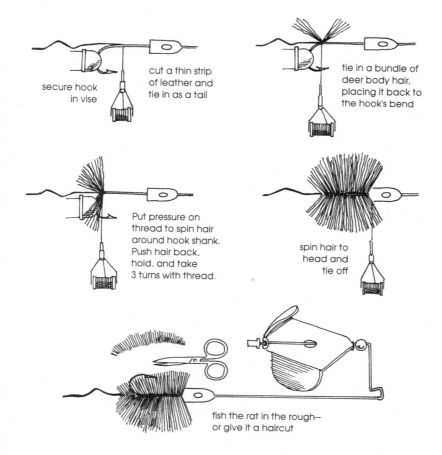

secure hook in vise

cut a thin strip of leather and tie in as a tail

tie in a bundle of deer body hair, placing it back to the hook's bend

Put pressure on thread to spin hair around hook shank. Push hair back, hold, and take 3 turns with thread.

spin hair to head and tie off

fish the rat in the rough-- or give it a haircut

out, almost at 90 degrees. This technique is called spinning.

After spinning the first batch of hair, push it back with your fingers (don't push the hair off the bend of the hook), and take a couple of turns with the thread immediately in front of the spun hair. Add another pinch of hair, spin it, and push it back tightly against the first bunch of hair. Repeat these steps until you have the hook full. Usually, you want as much hair as possible on the hook to give the rat buzz the proper proportion.

You can use exactly the same technique described above on spinnerbaits. Although I prefer the buzz model, I have tied spinnerbaits for anglers who fish them under the surface, using a single-spin. Such a bait can be deadly on largemouth. A rat tied onto a weedless jig can also be very good for fishing thick cover on bottom.

spin
rat

rat
jig

DOUBLE TROUBLE

Two lures rigged in tandem will often catch more fish than a single lure—and sometimes more than one kind of fish. Many anglers fish a small jig behind a larger jig. The larger jig is tied onto the fishing line as usual, then the end of a short piece of ordinary monofilament line is tied onto the larger jig's hook at the bend with a clinch knot, and the small jig is then tied onto the end of the short line. This simple rig will catch fish, but too often the line turns on the jig hook during the cast, causing the small jig to whip around and foul on the main jig or main line. The same thing can happen when the monofilament connector line is too long or limber.

This rig can be improved by trailing a lightweight fly instead of a small jig. The rig can be further improved by eliminating all the knots. Connect the fly and jig with nylon-coated steel leader material, wrapped onto both with fly-tying thread. For most fishing, a 15-pound leader will be about right. Don't use a leader that is too stiff, since a fish going after the larger jig will have to bend the leader out of the way before it can take the hook. After you have selected the right leader for your needs, proceed as follows:

1. Secure a hook with an up- or down-turned eye into a fly-tying vise. Wrap part of the shank with nylon thread. Cut a 7- or 8-inch length of plastic-coated leader material and insert one end through the hook's eye. Wrap the leader and hook shank together, tie off, and coat with head cement.

2. Tie a fly pattern of your choice. Most wet flies, streamers, and bucktails can be tied onto the hook. White bucktail is good for crappie, white, bass, and other fish that feed mostly on minnows. Tie in bucktail, hair, feathers, or other fly dressing materials directly over the hook shank and leader material. Steps 1 and 2 can be combined.

3. Remove the fly and clamp the jig hook into the vise. Wrap the hook's shank with thread. Cut the leader to length, place the end of the leader atop the hook shank, and wrap it tightly. Coat with head cement.

4. Dress the jig as usual with bucktail, Living Rubber, feathers, or material of your choice.

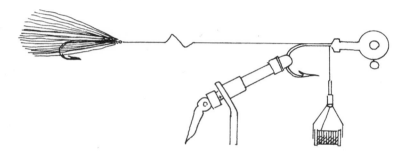

The choice of jig size and trailer hook size depends on what you're likely to catch, and on how far you expect to cast. For the small trailer lure, a white bucktail (maybe with a little flashy material added) about 1½ inches long tied onto a size 4 nickel-plated hook is ideal for white bass and crappie in most waters.

The main jig can be of any reasonable size, from ¼ ounce to 2 ounces, depending partly on how far you have to cast. For both stripers and hybrids, a white bucktail jig dressing from 3 to 4 inches long is hard to beat. Mylar

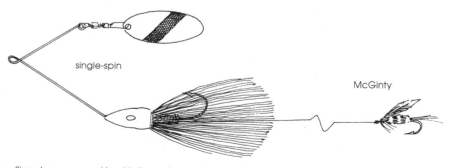

single-spin

McGinty

flies, streamers, and bucktails can be used on spinnerbaits and buzzbaits with hand-tied skirts or other flashy material can be tied in with the bucktail.

Some sort of double jig or jig and fly combination is fairly common. Here's a secret of mine: the same technique works even better with a spinnerbait and fly. Think about it. The slow fall of a single-spin, trailed by a fly (which tends to arc up), can be trouble for both bass and bluegills. Bluegills, I might add, are often attracted to spinnerbaits, but few are caught because of the small size of their mouth. A big one does get hooked from time to time, however, and the addition of a fly can be murder. The fly even takes some bass, too. For this combination, when the main targets are bass and bluegill, I prefer a black or brown fly. A little deer hair tied onto a hook and flared out somewhat will do fine. The basic rig is shown in the drawing on page 135.

TROLLING AIDS

Some time ago, Dan Gapen came out with a Bait Walker that could be used for trolling or for casting light baits. Basically, the rig was made with a spinnerbait wire with a coiled line-tie eyelet. The bottom weight was similar to a spinnerbait without a hook, and the top had a tightly closed loop for attaching a line. I think it also had a swivel in it. I have made pretty much the same rig by modifying a "walking sinker" mold (you can also use a spinnerbait mold). I prefer to reverse the wire, putting the long blade arm into the head and making a loop in the short arm. This rig is a great aid to trolling small in-line baits such as the Mepps without causing line twist. It can also be used for bottom bumping with a small floating plug, such as the Rapala, tied on with a foot or so of line.

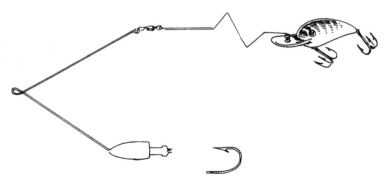

Remove hook and blades from long-armed spinnerbait.
Tie a suitable lure to swivel and troll.

SINKERS

Anyone who invests in a lead pot should also look at the various sinker molds on the market. Molds for egg sinkers, worm sinkers, pyramid sinkers, and many others are available, including some for specialty trolling rigs.

Most sinkers are easy to pour, and a reject isn't a big deal because the whole thing is simply melted again. Thus, lead or one of the new nontoxic alloys that don't work well for pouring spinnerbaits and buzzbaits can often be "used up" in sinkers.

Be warned, however, that lead sinkers are on the way out. They have already been banned in England, and in this country the Environmental Protection Agency (EPA) is expected to limit the use of lead. The problem, they say, is that birds eat, or "ingest," lead sinkers and die.

At this writing, it is unclear exactly what will be banned and where. What is the maximum size sinker that birds can ingest? I may be wrong, but it's unlikely that the first round of regulations from the EPA will make the matter crystal clear; I'd guess that anyone who expects to understand exactly what's what will need a law degree and a working knowledge of Federal Prose. Meanwhile, some sinker manufacturers are switching to alloys of one sort or another. One smelter I know of is currently using a mixture of tin and bismuth, both of which have low melting points. Another manufacturer (I was told) has gone to zinc, calling the result *zinkers*. Of course, zinkers may be more dangerous than ordinary sinkers. No doubt the EPA will be charged with determining which elements are unsafe to use in sinkers and which are not. And sinker alloys for the do-it-yourselfer will surely become available in time, so don't throw out your sinker molds.

Whether or not the new no-lead law will be expanded to include fishing lures remains to be seen. At present, the argument is that birds ingest the lead, not that lead leaches out and poisons the water. In this context, it would be difficult to ban lead for spinnerbaits and buzzbaits simply because birds don't swallow them—but strange things happen in politics, newsmaking, the tackle business, TV fishing shows, and advertising. My admittedly cynical guess is that an expansion of the law to ban any use of lead in fishing tackle will be supported and perhaps even instigated by the larger firms that traffic in spinnerbaits, buzzbaits, and jigs. Why? It will give them an opportunity to increase prices and at the same time knock out (or at least stun) the nagging competition from hundreds of small manufacturers and thousands of hobbyists around the country.

Frankly, the whole thing strikes me as un-American. Can you imagine Tom Sawyer fishing with a bismuth sinker?

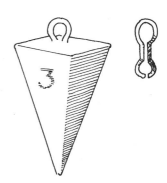

molds for making dozens of sinkers are available, as well as eyelets and other hardware

Fishing with Leadheads

Chapter

14

Because it's difficult for me to discuss the design of some leadheads without also discussing how they should be fished, some of the material in this chapter has already been covered. A recap might be in order here in case the main purpose of the lure might have become lost in a discussion of wire angles and other fine points, but I'll try to keep it short:

BUZZBAITS

All buzzbaits are designed to be fished on top of the water, usually when the fish are feeding in shallow water. The buzzbait's main feature is the rhythmic sound made by the large blade slapping and churning the surface of the water. Buzzbaits are usually fished with a slow, steady retrieve—as a rule, the slower the retrieve better. To achieve a slow retrieve, use the largest possible blade with the smallest (lightest) head that will keep the bait up and tracking straight. There are limits in either direction, and, in my opinion, some people put too much weight in the head, resulting in a lure that will run straight. The do-it-yourselfer may opt for a lighter head or a larger blade, knowing that the lure will run to one side or the other if it is snaked in.

I confess again, however, that I sometimes like to fish rather fast even though I am aware that slowing down might result in catching more fish. In order to fish faster, I sometimes rig a small buzz blade on a heavy head. I call it a jerk buzz, and I work it across the surface with quick sweeps of the rod tip, quickly reeling in the slack during the brief pause between jerks. I like to think that this bait resembles a wounded fish fluttering on top. Sometimes frisky bass agree with me, or at least think it's something struggling along on the surface.

As a rule, however, buzzbaits are retrieved slow and steady, and their noise makes them ideal for fishing in muddy water where visibility might be a problem. Bass and other gamefish can home in on such baits. The noise made by the blade also makes them ideal for fishing at night, and the steady plop-plop-plop helps the angler stay in touch with the lure.

I almost always prefer a single blade to a double blade, but there are other opinions on this. Beyond doubt, however, single-blade baits cast better and are easier to store in a tackle box. Double-spins, if rigged with right- and left-turning blades, do track much better than single-blade lures.

Buzzbaits can be fished effectively in rivers, but they're primarily lures for ponds and lakes. In large lakes and impoundments, they can be very effective on the flats. On Lake Weir in Florida, where I once lived on an island, there was a vast area behind my house that was about 4 or 5 feet deep with about 3 feet of moss on the bottom. A buzzbait was ideal for fishing there at night and on cloudy days. Very large bass also moved about in this area during the spawning period.

Finally, let me say that buzzbaits are usually more effective for largemouth bass than for other species of gamefish.

TANDEM SPINNERBAITS

These lures are my favorites for the ordinary cast-and-retrieve routine. It's hard to go wrong with tandem-spins, provided you present the bait in a reasonable manner, close to the fish. They are not ideal as fall baits or for bouncing along the bottom, but they can be used either way. I have caught fish by sticking a long plastic worm or pork eel onto the hook, without dressing, and fishing it very slowly on the bottom.

Tandem-spins are usually more effective in shallow water, and in $\frac{1}{8}$-, $\frac{1}{4}$-, or $\frac{3}{8}$-ounce weights. Rigged with large blades and fished rather fast, so that they make a wake just under the surface of the water, these baits are ideal for burbling. There's a fine line between a wake and a burble (a burble is a fast wake with a few bubbles made as the blade chops the surface), and either method will take fish, especially lunker largemouth. If you're making a wake in thin grass and see another wake coming, hold on.

SINGLE-SPINS

These baits can be fished on or very near the surface, bounced along the bottom, or fished anywhere in between. Single-spins are, in fact, the most versatile lure ever invented. They are ideal for fishing as a fall bait, as discussed at some length in the first chapter, and they will do things for the angler that are difficult to achieve with other baits. First, the blade slows down the fall rate. Second, the blade's vibration keeps the angler in touch with his lure and signals a "strike" when the vibration stops. This second point requires not only a perfectly designed and rigged spinnerbait but also the proper fishing line and a sensitive rod—and concentration. The technique is not for everybody, but it's the secret of some anglers who seem to catch more than their share of big bass on spinnerbaits.

Some of the really big bass caught by "slow rolling" are taken from rather deep water—30 or 40 feet. Once the bait is down, it's fished by lifting the rod tip and then following it back down with the rod tip. Carl Wingo, a deepwater sport from Virginia, has taken lots of big bass with this technique, and he confessed to me that he uses his electric fishing motor to move about over a hotspot instead of making repeated casts. He has even been known to fish in this manner from a pontoon boat instead of his bassboat. Carl prefers ¾- or 1-ounce baits for slow rolling.

Single-spins are also good for fishing as a fall bait in rather shallow water, or along ledges. When casting to cover, such as lily pads, try casting into a pocket or likely spot, retrieving to the edge, and letting the bait sink, tight-lining as you go. Watch your line like a hawk. If it twitches, jerk.

As a rule, fishing in medium-depth or shallow water is best done with a smaller bait; I like the ¼-ounce size fitted with a size 3½ Colorado blade. In grass, I like to fish a ⅛-ounce bait with a size 4 willowleaf blade. As a rule, I rig a single-spin with a snap swivel, which makes it easy to switch blades.

IN-LINE SPINNERBAITS

Some of these spinnerbaits are popular for casting to heavy cover, usually in shallow water. As a rule, they cast into brush better than any of the safety-pin designs. The long rabbit-ear weedguard on some baits, however, is not ideal for casting into brush.

Of course, in-line baits such as the Mepps, often dressed with treble hooks, are fished in lakes and streams at various depths for various species of freshwater fish. Line twist is sometimes a problem with these lures, but their overall effectiveness for catching a wide range of fish is beyond question.

Weight-forward in-line baits, such as the Eerie Deerie, are popular for fishing deep for walleye and other bottom huggers. These will also catch other fish, shallow or deep, and the weight-forward keel design helps prevent line twist. They are, however, easy for a jumping, head-shaking fish to throw back at you.

JIGS

To describe every possible way to fish a jig would require another book. They're good for casting long distances, especially if sparsely dressed, and for fishing on bottom. For vertical fishing, a properly dressed center-weighted jig has a unique minnowlike action.

When fishing on bottom, think about crawfish. The jig should be weedless and dressed like something that feeds on or scoots along the bottom.

For open water, it's usually best to think in terms of baitfish for ideas about designing, dressing, and fishing jigs. In my opinion, we should use the concept of swimming eels more often in our fishing. A curl-tailed worm attached to a pointed jig head and fished with a steady retrieve can be deadly on black bass—and on stripers. Don't tell anybody, but one of the most productive lures I've ever fished was a ¹⁄₁₆-ounce long-nose jig on a number 8 hook dressed with a thin, 4-inch wavy-tail worm, rigged in nonweedless fashion and fished with ultralight spinning gear.

OTHER LEADHEADS

Most of the other leadhead lures are good for making long casts or for fishing in very deep water. Often, lead minnows are ideal for schooling fish that are feeding on shad or other baitfish. Sometimes you have to match the hatch almost exactly, so that you'll need a lead minnow of the right size.

Lead spoons are also good for making long casts, and for jigging vertically in deep water. Try free-spooling one down beside standing trees in large impoundments. Typically, these are worked down to the bottom, then jigged up and down. Usually, the strikes will come on the fall.

The sonic vibrators are great lures for taking schooling fish in open water, and I like to fish them on a throw-and-retrieve, fan-cast basis. They cast like a bullet, and, on the retrieve, they make a vibration that the angler can feel. I always like a bait that talks to me.

Epilogue from the Bay Window

"It's a damned lie," I said, shoving the magazine across the table. As usual, my wife and I were having breakfast coffee at our favorite nook beside the bay window, through which we enjoyed the morning view of our cypress pond.

"What now?" she asked, as though she had already heard everything. "Look at that blue heron——"

"It's Berkley. That ad," I said almost at a loss for words. "They've come out with a newfangled spinnerbait and they stuck one of those hazardous signs in the magazine advertisement, implying that ordinary leadheads are dangerous. Look at that." I reached out and put my finger on the symbol in the full-page advertisement.

"Well . . . ?" she asked.

"I'm going to write a letter——" I said.

"What about lead shot and ducks?" she asked.

"What about 'em? Look, a fish is not going to swallow a spinnerbait like a duck swallows birdshot. I've never in my life seen a fish with a lead lure in its belly. Not even a jig, much less a spinnerbait or a buzzbait. It's a goddamned lie, I tell you."

"I believe you, I believe you," she said, throwing up her hands. "But lead *is* soluble in water, is it not?"

"Maybe if drinking water stands in pipes . . . but there's a good deal of difference between the volume of water carried by a 1-inch pipe and the Tennessee River. This would be easy enough to test. Each large impoundment has a ton of leadhead jigs in the rocks below the dam. Somebody ought to test the water for lead at the beginning and end of a tailrace."

"Did you see that?" she asked, trying to change the subject and pointing toward the blue heron, which stood on one leg and looked at us. A bass had swirled the water near a hollow cypress stump just a good casting distance from the bank.

"I see lead," I said, then drank off the last of my coffee. "Actually," I went on, "lead has got to be somewhere. Maybe we would be better off if we dumped all of it into Lake Eufaula. That way, the Chattahoochee will cover the lead up with dirt from the hills of Georgia within a few years. Meanwhile, it would be safe from the goddamn birds."

"Look, A. D.," she said, raising her hackles a bit, "just because you have written a book on spinnerbaits doesn't necessarily make them safe to use."

"Well, maybe not," I allowed. "But I'll tell you what, Sassafras. I'll take you out to dinner and ask my publisher to drop future printings of the book when and if any Federal agency passes a readable law prohibiting the use of spinnerbaits and other leadhead lures in our waters. [We'll just make A. D. figure out how to mold heads from nontoxic alloys. Eds.] Meanwhile, I would hope that Berkley, if they really believe leadhead spinnerbaits are hazardous, would surely take ultralight Trilene and other monofilament fishing line off the market until more drastic steps can be taken."

"Oh?" She smiled at me. "On what grounds?"

"Obviously, Berkley wouldn't want people fishing such dangerous lures on ultralight monofilament, which is easy to break off even if the lure isn't thrown into the top of a cypress tree and even if the line doesn't have over-hand knots in it or nicks on it. I would think that any monofilament under 17-pound test ought to be called back in, pending a ruling on the lead-lure controversy. Furthermore," I went on, "I would suggest that Berkley suspend all production of monofilament of all sizes until they come up with a more biodegradable material and a spinning reel that doesn't cause bird's nests. That's a good name, I might add. Bird and animal lovers will agree with what I'm saying." I looked out the window, adding, "Ain't that right, Blue Heron?" The fish swirled again beside the hollow stump.

"You've got a good point," she said.

"Also," I went on, pushing my advantage, "I would expect Berkley to get out of the plastic worm business as soon as possible. I've caught too many large bass that had swallowed plastic worms. Gut hooked. There ought to be a law against it. I said this back in 1971, when writing *Fishing for Bass*. Do you remember——"

"I remember," she said, pushing her chair away from the table. "Before you get started on the Texas rig again, let's go fish for a few minutes. I'll promise to take that plastic worm off my rod and tie on one of your precious hand-tied spinnerbaits." She stood behind my chair and put her hands on the back of my neck.

"Can I tie the knot?" I asked.

"Yes," she said.

"Then let's do it," I said, getting up just as a much larger bass broke the water near the stump, making waves and frightening the blue heron. "I'll write the letter when we get back."

A. D. Livingston

Sources of Materials, Components, and Tools

Appendix

Al's Goldfish Lure Co., P.O. Box 51013, Indian Orchard, MA 01151. Al's offers a limited line of Colorado blades, propeller blades, swing blades, and what they call a continental blade, which has an elongated oval shape. They also have casting spoons and various lure components, including a line of plastic plug bodies, and a limited line of wire, jigs, leadheads, and in-line lure bodies. All items are sold in bulk, intended for manufacturers.

Angler's Workshop, P.O. Box 1010, Woodland, WA 98674. Heavy on rod-building blanks, tools, and materials, this firm also sells fly-tying and luremaking components.

Barlow's Tackle Shop, P.O. Box 830369, Richardson, TX 75083. This firm carries a complete line of tools and materials for the luremaker, fly tyer, and tackle tinkerer. Also known as Limit Manufacturing Company, or Limit for short, it's probably the largest supplier for the do-it-yourselfer.

Bass Pro Shops, 1935 South Campbell, Springfield, MO 65898. This large mail-order house offers blades, swivels, and other lure components.

Bead Tackle Company, 65 Holland Avenue, Bridgeport, CT 06605. Bead chains and Lunker rigging systems.

Billy Henry, Inc., 3305 S. Route 31, Crystal Lake, IL 60014. Plastic spinner blades, 3-wing plastic buzz blades, and Y-guard weedguards.

Blade Tackle & Sporting Goods, 2103 33rd Street, Erie, PA 16510. Lure components, soft plastic, and other items.

Cabela's, Inc., 812 13th Avenue, Sidney, NE 69160. A complete line of fishing and sporting equipment, with several catalog pages devoted to luremaking components.

Carolina Novelty Co., 10526 Brief Road, Charlotte, NC 28227. Luremakers' supplies.

Cast Industries, P.O. Box 7468, Springfield, IL 62791. Centrifugal molds for jigs, spinnerbaits, buzzbaits, and other leadheads. They also sell bulk leadheads, painted or raw.

Cind-Al Mfg., 13518 Granville Avenue, Clermont, FL 34711. Precision molds for spinnerbaits, buzzbaits, jigs, and other leadheads, along with custom molds for soft plastics.

Component Systems, 5003 Packer Drive, Wausau, WI 54401. Vinyl-lure and jig paint.

Conley Casting Supply Corp., 124 Maple Street, Warwick, RI 02888. Centrifugal casting supplies and equipment, new and used.

Custom Tackle Supply, 2559 Highway 41-A South, Shelbyville, TN 37160. Wholesale lure components, molds, fly-tying materials, tools, and rod-building components.

Do-It Molds, 501 State Street, Denver, IA 50622. This firm manufactures a large number of molds for jigs, spinnerbaits, and other lures as well as sinkers for do-it-yourselfers and small manufacturers. They also carry blades, swivels, and other components as well as lure paints.

Fish Hair Enterprises, Inc., 1484 West County Road C., St. Paul, MN 55113. Synthetic hair, rubber skirt material (called Real Rubber), thread, and other materials. Wholesale and bulk.

Gander Mountain, Inc., Box 248, Hwy. W, Wilmot, WI 53192. Full-line outdoor equipment supplier, with a good selection of luremaking components.

Frank Hauck's Living Rubber Components, P.O. Box 336, Byron, CA 94514. Geared to servicing large and small manufacturers as well as wholesalers, Frank Hauck's offers a complete line of Living Rubber as well as the DuPont Lumaflex skirt material.

Hagen's, Rt. 2, Box 82, Mitchell, SD 57301. At one time, this company made blades and lure components for the old Herter's and other companies. They now offer a complete line of spinner blades, spoon blanks, and leadheads, including jigs, spinnerbaits, and buzzbaits. Other products include wire, swivels, in-line lure bodies, slip-on skirts, hooks, and so on.

E. Hille, P.O. Box 996, Williamsport, PA 17703. Mail-order components for luremakers and rod builders.

Hobbs Feather Co., Inc., Selling wholesale and bulk, Hobbs provides a wide variety of feathers, hair, and other products that can be used on spinnerbaits. They also market skirts and skirt material, which they call Lure-Fil.

Hedron, Inc., 402 N. Main Street, Stillwater, MN 55082. Flashabou and other lure dressing materials.

Jann's, P.O. Box 4315, Toledo, OH 43609. This mail-order firm offers a complete line of components for luremakers and rod builders.

Jerry's Tackle Shop, 604 12th Street, Highland, IL 62249. Mail-order materials and components for lures and flies.

Kayser Lure Corp., P.O. Box 68, Ursa, IL 62376. Skirt materials, tools, and custom weedguards.

Lakeland Incorporated, One Lakeland Drive, Isle, MN 56342. A major supplier for manufacturers and distributors, this firm offers a complete line of spinner blades, preformed wire, in-line lure bodies, and spoon blanks. They also market Eagle Claw hooks and other items used on lures, and they market spinnerbait and buzzbait heads.

Land-O-Tackle, Inc., 3206 Nordic Road, Arlington Heights, IL 60005. Lure components and custom-made molds for injection molding.

Mid Atlantic Tackle Co., 50-0 Corbin Avenue, Bayshore, NY 11706. Bulk heads for spinnerbaits, buzzbaits, and jigs. Also, custom casting and molds for centrifugal casting.

Midland Tackle Co., 66 Route 17, Sloatsburg, NY 10974. Molds, wire, hooks, spinner blades, wire benders, and other tools and materials for luremakers.

Molds, 514 Chelsea Street, Hot Springs, AR 71901. Since 1960, this company has been making small molds for jigs, spinnerbaits, buzzbaits, and other leadheads. They specialize in custom work in aluminum alloy, and they may be able to produce a mold to your specifications. They usually require a sample.

Mustang Wire Products, Inc., P. O. Box 53, Mustang, OK 73064. This firm specializes in stainless steel wire, and they offer custom service as well as standard sizes and shapes for spinnerbaits and buzzbaits. They say that no minimum order is required—but they add that items must be purchased in lots of 1,000. I have never used their wire, but the samples that I have look good and have tight bends, which I favor, up to a point.

Netcraft, 2800 Tremainsville Road, Toledo, OH 43613. Supplies and tools for making lures, nets, rods, and other fishing tackle.

Proto Products Company, 6830 W. State, Milwaukee, WI 53213. Proto Products sells centrifugal casting equipment and specializes in making custom molds for use on this equipment. They also make fixtures for soldering ice-fishing lures.

Quality Tackle Co., P.O. Box 162, Nashotah, WI 53058. Molds, wire, hooks, and other materials for luremakers. Discount program for large orders.

Rat Trap Bait Co., Inc., P.O. Box 845, Auburndale, FL 33823. This company makes a lot of the slip-on skirts for the tackle industry. These include several sizes and kinds of rubber, silicone, and Lumaflex skirts.

Raymond C. Rumpf & Son, P.O. Box 319, Sellersville, PA 18960. A wholesaler, Rumpf & Son carries lure components, fly-tying materials, Living Rubber, tools, and so on. They have minimum orders and do not cater to individual do-it-yourselfers.

RM Engineered Products, Inc., P.O. Box 5202, North Charleston, SC 29406. Silicone skirts.

Rosco, P.O. Box 109, Rome, NY 13440. A division of Rome Specialty Company, Inc., Rosco manufactures and markets a line of swivels, snaps, snap swivels, split rings, and other components. They also manufacture a wide range of leader sleeves, which can be used as spacers on spinnerbaits. I like their stainless steel Duo-lock snaps.

Shorty's Hook Sales, Inc., 202 County Line Road, Windsor, MO 65360. Bulk hooks, including Eagle Claw, VMC, and Mustad.

Sampo, P.O. Box 328, Barneveld, NY 13304. Ball-bearing swivels, available with two split rings, one ring and a snap, or with neither ring nor snap.

Sunkeye Heads, Route 3, Box 19, Headland, AL 36345. Spinnerbait heads (from 1/8 to 1 ounce), buzzbait heads, and V-guard weedless jigs. Also, hand-held wire benders for forming loops in the end of the spinnerbait arm. Retail and wholesale. If you don't want to make your own heads, this is a good place to get them.

Sweet's Molds, P.O. Box 127, Springville, NY 14141. Molds.

Tackle-Craft, P.O. Box 280, Chippewa Falls, WI 54729. Materials, supplies, and equipment for making jigs, flies, spinnerbaits, and other lures.

Venom Mfg. & Dist. Company, P.O. Box 275, Lithopolis, OH 43136. Soft plastics and glass "worm rattles." Custom lead and plastic molding.

Wapsi, Route 5, Box 57E, Mountain Home, AR 72653. Wholesale fly-tying materials and tools.

Worth Manufacturing Company, P.O. Box 88, Stevens Point, WI 54481. Bulk sales for manufacturers. Spinner blades, wire, split rings, and other components. Also, wire-forming tools and split-ring pliers.

Index